A t

MANHEIMER, Ronald J. Kierkegaard as educator. California, 1978 (c1977). 218p index 76-24587. 11.50 ISBN 0-520-03312-4
The title of this book may mislead the reader expecting some theory of education drawn from Kierkegaard's writings. Manheimer, in fact, does not proceed to any general conclusions. He makes a careful survey of the material in Kierkegaard's authorship relative to the teacher, the learner, and the limits of communication, seeking to show the significance of this material in the context of Kierkegaard's dialectical thinking. In so doing, he makes a substantial contribution to the interpretation of individual works, particularly *Either/Or* and *Works of love*. Thus, *Kierkegaard as educator* will be of immediate interest to all students of Kierkegaard and will supplement such more comprehensive studies as Gregor Malantschuk's *Kierkegaard's thought* (CHOICE, June 1972) and Mark C. Taylor's *Kierkegaard's pseudonymous authorship: a study of time and the self* (CHOICE, Nov. 1975). It will also be a useful source for those concerned with the philosophy of language.

D1154324

Kierkegaard as Educator

KIERKEGAARD
AS
EDUCATOR

Ronald J. Manheimer

UNIVERSITY OF CALIFORNIA PRESS

Berkeley   Los Angeles   London

University of California Press
Berkeley and Los Angeles, California

University of California Press, Ltd.
London, England

In memory of my father,
Irving Nathan Manheimer
(1908—1975)

Contents

Acknowledgments

The first version of this book was written in the long winter and late spring of 1971 in northwest Jutland, Denmark. A farmhouse beside the Limfjord in the county of Thy was part of the setting. There my wife Caroline and I had been staff members of an association of small residential colleges devoted to innovation in multi-cultural higher education, the Nordenfjord World University. My interests in Kierkegaard's conception of human development and in the possibilities of educative situations intersected in the process of working out what was then a doctoral dissertation for The History of Consciousness program at the University of California, Santa Cruz. The Danforth Foundation helped to make this period possible. Caroline Manheimer's willingness to read my words back to me with critical sensitivity helped make it actual. The staff at the little town of Thisted's fine library, where I found a first edition of Kierkegaard's *Either/Or*, also assisted me. Angela West gave strong editorial support. Christy Bidstrup typed the manuscript. And Professor Albert Hofstadter saw me through to the completion of a work entitled "Kierkegaard and the Education of Historical Consciousness" (Ph.D. dissertation, University of California, Santa Cruz, 1973).

In the spring of 1974, while I was visiting lecturer at the

University of California in Santa Cruz, Dr. Sherri Peiros, then a graduate student, read the dissertation and encouraged me to share it more widely. Helpful comments from one of my reviewers, Professor Barbara Anderson, author of *Kierkegaard: A Fiction* (Syracuse: Syracuse University Press, 1974), lead to a reconceiving of the dissertation which eventually issued in the form of the present work.

I am grateful to Cindy Haupt and Karen Reubel, part of the secretarial staff of the philosophy department at San Diego State University, for typing the new version. My thanks also go to Robert Y. Zachary, of the University of California Press, for his encouragement through the last two years of this long process.

Several past teachers have been seminal in my formulation of this book. They are Professor George Drury, formerly of Monteith College, Wayne State University, and now at Empire State College, New York; Aage Rosendal Nielson, Rector, New Experimental College, Denmark; and my thesis advisor, Professor Albert Hofstadter, formerly of the University of California, Santa Cruz, and now at the New School for Social Research, New York. The germination of thought which this book reflects is my own version of the Socratic manner of teaching I found in these three educators.

R. J. M.

Introduction

Kierkegaard employed a variety of styles and a host of pseudonyms to engage the interest of his readers. He published,
simultaneously, religious, philosophical, psychological, and
even humorous books and all within incredibly short periods.
To the concerned reader, this many sided authorship can
seem bafflingly complex, involving him in an intricate and
subtle dialectic of viewpoints. Kierkegaard's authorship embodies a multiplicity of voices aimed to reach the concrete
reality of the reader as existing in the midst of a way of life.
Like a good novelist Kierkegaard strives not only to depict
but to project forms of life that reach out to the reader—a
reader recognized as one whose wholeness of being is itself
made up of a plurality of dimensions of experience and meaning. The individual's being is his activity as a person in process of integrating complex forces into a unity. An authorship
that recognizes that the being of the individual is in his becoming, will require of itself appropriate forms of communication. The wealth of forms of communication distinguishes
Kierkegaard as a brilliant stylist. But his style is not merely
ornamental or rhetorical; it is a movement of thought in language designed to enable the reader to make use of his own
capabilities for personal appropriation. Thus, by drawing the
reader reflectively out into the light of personal possibility,

Kierkegaard's authorship is an educative one. By reflecting back upon itself the very difficulty of this process, his is a doubly reflective authorship whose educative function points to the possibilities and limits of what it means to educate.

Kierkegaard is not usually associated with a particular system or philosophy of education. He has, in fact, written comparatively little in the way of direct commentary on the content of education. But, through his authorship, he has sought to educate the reader indirectly through conjoining the *what* and the *how* of existence by interrelating the content and form of his communication. He stands in the tradition of great teachers such as Socrates, Augustine, Pascal, Nietzche, and Wittgenstein for whom saying is also, ideally, a form of doing, and for whom doing means to awaken the individual to possibilities of self-transformation. Unique to this tradition of thinkers who could communicate possibility is the intense, often passionate awareness of the forms that language must take if it is to speak to the inner person. Correspondingly, common to such thinkers is the knowledge that to bring a person to his own possibilities requires simultaneously to bring him to consciousness of his limitations. Socrates does this through the irony that exposes the individual to his own ignorance. Only by first arriving at the impasse of self-contradiction does the person identify difficulties that can become points of departure for self-discovery. The same could be said for the others, however differently they approach the individual and bring him to the initiation of self-inquiry. Strangely, the more evident the content of such transformations in these thinkers, to that extent are their methods of enabling us increasingly opaque. And this is equally true of Kierkegaard's ability to educate.

Perhaps it will seem confusing to use the word "educate" in relationship to Kierkegaard's authorship, since, most commonly, education refers to institutionally related learning in which knowledge gets transferred from teacher to student. Someone might urge us that the term education as used here might better be replaced by something like self-discovery or

self-actualization. Furthermore, it is true that Kierkegaard
would have disdained being called an educator as he would
have understood the term. Nevertheless, the value of Kierkegaard's many sided authorship, with its increasingly interiorized forms of address, is precisely that it brings into question fundamental assumptions about a range of educative
intentions. These intentions to educate may vary from the
formal classroom situation to the informal conversations of
friends, lovers, and colleagues. Whenever one person turns
to another in anticipation of playing a role in that person's
development (becoming), there is the intention to educate.
The word educate, in the context of this book, may mean to
enable, to help, to awaken, or even to edify. Hopefully the
reader can tolerate this degree of generality. It is done for the
sake of illuminating what is common to intentions to educate
and for the sake of evoking fundamental assumptions related
to acts furthering possibilities of human development.

The educative possibilities of Kierkegaard's authorship
have attracted many scholars and students into their depths.
The reader has only to refer to the bibliographies of secondary works on Kierkegaard to appreciate the vast number
and variety of contributions.[1] Among these, quite recently,
have appeared several very good if not excellent works seeking to unravel the complexity of the pseudonymous narrators
behind the many sides of the authorship.[2] Still, it is important to remember that Kierkegaard regarded his authorship
as his own education. And while I join the ranks of Kierkegaard scholars, hoping to make a worthwhile contribution to
this effort, I must admit that I have allowed myself the opportunity to seek to join Kierkegaard's process of self-education
with my own and to let myself be moved "by the waters of
language" in the authorship and to reflect, in the pages that
follow, aspects of my own self-education. I believe that this is
consistent with the authorship's attempt to call forth the
reader, and I only wish that my "existential response" were
more adequate to the challenge.

This book, about the education of possibility and the confrontation with limits, will explicate, discuss, and evoke a dialectic of education in Kierkegaard's many sided authorship. In it I will not try to explain the function of all the pseudonyms and how, taken together, they constitute a single plan, nor will I reveal much about Kierkegaard's equally complicated life. Instead, in a threefold approach, I will be engaged with aspects of the authorship having to do with education, communication, and language as they involve possibilities and limits of self-transformation and as the authorship itself reflects these themes back upon itself. I feel that I owe it to the reader to make this enterprise as clear as possible from the outset since it will be easy to get lost (hopefully to good avail) once under way. Furthermore, since this book has no final conclusory chapter, I would like to share my incomplete conclusions with the reader right from the start, that these may serve the reader to find his bearing and hold it throughout the meanderings of this voyage.

This book traces Kierkegaard's authorship to three limits. First, in Part I, it follows a series of interpretations of the Socratic educator. Increasingly, Kierkegaard came to see a deepened human act in the possibilities that could be shared between teacher and learner, between man and man; I call these his "Socratic postures." The way in which Kierkegaard understands the stance of the teacher and the situation of the learner parallels the strategy of his different forms of discourse. Intrinsic to this design is the limit Kierkegaard himself designates for what can occur between human beings, and what can occur only between a man and his God. But while there may be limits or boundaries between human and divine education, the conceptions of these bear significantly upon one another. Two teachers, Socrates and Christ, draw closer together in Kierkegaard's understanding of educating possibility. While at least three versions of Socratic postures emerge in Part I, the conclusion I come to is that the authorship, taken as Kierkegaard's dialectic of education, remains poised at the threshold where the Socratic and Christian meet. This meeting does serve to sustain the dialectic. But it also leaves us with a question: Must Kierkegaard always stand indirectly related to the reader through the deceptive guise of his Socratic smile? Correspondingly, must the one who teaches, who enables the learner, always remain remote from the shared possibilities of reciprocal responsibility?

I do not think that I ever finally answer the question of Kierkegaardian limits. Yet each of the three parts of this book moves precisely toward the same issue. The second part begins as if from the beginning again by entering into the dialectic of possibility which makes Kierkegaard's early and popular book, *Either/Or*, a drama of education. While Part I approaches a Socratic education through historical and conceptual issues such as Hegel's interpretation of Socrates, the concept of becoming, Socratic irony, comic consciousness and the notion of the witness, Part II explores the dramatic character of *Either/Or*'s two antiheroes, known only to us as A and B (though B is sometimes referred to as Judge William). Kierkegaard gets two radically different ways of life mirrored into one another without resolving these reflections into a single image. The inconclusiveness of *Either/Or* tends to draw the reader in as adjudicator between A and B, only to mirror the reader back upon himself. Some readers of this book may find Part II a more accessible entry point and they are invited to begin there.

Part II focuses on the role of moral education as one that calls for self-transformation through the act of "choosing oneself." This imperative, "Choose yourself," is addressed by B to his younger contemporary, the melancholy and poetic A. It is B who introduces the notion that mythology, history, and human individuation can be divided into stages of development expressive of life attitudes. The important role played by a theory of life stages as conceived by the moral educator is extended beyond the explicit scope of Kierkegaard's dialectic of education. How one perceives his own and others' development may help or hinder his ability to participate in that life process. Out of the context of *Either/Or*, the helper's need to help is examined. While again there is no one final conclusion to Part II, the issues are, I believe, sharpened. The intention to educate, which now includes an awareness of life stages, is reformulated according to a theory of "positional" and "situational" consciousness.

Life stages reveal the individual as fundamentally rooted in a way of life. The communication across and between ways of life becomes the focus of Part III. The thesis and theme of Part III is that to enable is to communicate possibility. We do not exactly start over again but now draw on Parts I and II to crystallize the educative dialectic of possibility and limit as communicating interpretations of existence. In this third thematic exploration, the emergent picture of human development is transformed, as Kierkegaard transformed it, into a theory of the variety of human discourse. To educate as to communicate possibility is searched out in Kierkegaard's dialectic of communication. Edification, metaphorical speech, the language of love and its limits form the context where the boundaries of Kierkegaard's teaching and authorship are again critically encountered. In his doctrine of the love of the neighbor we can see Kierkegaard's whole authorship in retrospect. The same problem remains. When does it become appropriate for the dialectic of possibility to become actualized in the mutual accessibility of true reciprocity? While the work ends with this question still posed, one general conclusion may be stated. Kierkegaard's authorship has much to teach us about self-knowledge, about writing and speech, about communication that transforms us as both speakers and listeners, as authors and interpreters. His work stands as a momentous contribution especially for those whose vocation involves the intention to educate, where educating takes place fundamentally through language—through the communication of possibility.

PART I

Educating Subjectivity:
Kierkegaard's Three Socratic Postures

It may truly be said that there is something Socratic about me.

—KIERKEGAARD, *Papirer*, 1849

Preface

In order to understand Kierkegaard as educator it is necessary to follow his interpretation of Socrates. The character of Socrates and those exhibited principles that we call the Socratic were of the utmost concern to Kierkegaard in formulating his position as thinker, author, and religious individual. In Socrates the activities of educating, thinking, and doing were united. He was for Kierkegaard the paradigm of that fully human being whom Kierkegaard would call *Hiin Enkelte*, "the individual." In his understanding and depiction of Socrates Kierkegaard gathered every major aspect of his philosophical and religious points of view. What is of crucial importance for us is that Kierkegaard's foremost instance of authentic being was contained in the figure of an educative thinker whom Kierkegaard would describe as that "existing subjective thinker."[1]

Kierkegaard's portrayal of Socrates focuses upon *how* Socrates engages others in philosophical discourse. The inward dimension of that relationship toward his pupils is characterized by seeing Socrates as fundamentally rooted in a process of self-development, which Kierkegaard calls a "mission."[2] For Kierkegaard, Socrates is essentially in a process of "becoming," and that is what makes him "existential" and makes him available to the life of any other thinker who relates self-development to self-knowledge as a personal appropriation.

As a significant undertaking, to grasp Kierkegaard's "existential Socrates," our efforts are also formidable. There is not one interpretation of Socrates to contend with but numerous and sometimes conflicting ones. In his most sustained advance upon the Socratic, which is to be found in one of the earliest works, his *magister* dissertation *Concept of Irony*, Kierkegaard introduces us to his educative mentor by saying that efforts to describe Socrates are as "baffling as trying to depict an elf wearing a hat that makes him invisible."[3] Hence, the reader is forewarned that this is going to be an exercise in invisibility. But the difficulties of undertaking this formidable task are also opportunities for illuminating Kierkegaard's activity as a philosophic and religious author, his models for educating an awareness of human singularity, the relationship between educator and pupil, and for gaining an initial impression of what Kierkegaard means by "life attitudes" (*livs-anskuelser*) or, as he also calls them, "life stages."

The variety of interpretations which Kierkegaard makes of Socrates over the span of his authorship can be apprehended in several ways. First, they indicate Kierkegaard's own maturing view of *how* Socrates participated in the life of thought as an existing thinker. By implication this offers some insight into transformations in Kierkegaard's own personal life. Second, the interpretations are couched in the language of Kierkegaard's notion of life atitudes—comprehensive life modalities through which an individual bestows value, meaning, and significance on experience. By following the developing view of Socrates' various postures as educator, we are following a depiction of human development in which an increasingly more mature position is attained. These positions have deep influence on the formulation that Kierkegaard would give to his own educative enterprise, his "authorship." Third, the Socratic postures could be understood less as a sequence of surpassed life-attitudes than as a set of transformations which refer back and forth to one another in presenting dimensions of a multifaceted educative thinker who must be grasped from more than one perspective.

Our present approach emphasizes the second and third possible understanding of Kierkegaard's Socrates, foregoing the biographical account that might have been rendered. We seek to explore the relationship between particular characterizations of the Socratic educative postures and the form of self-knowledge which animates these orientations. This should throw light on first, the relationship between the educator's idea of educating and his conception of what it means to be an individual; second, the implications for a philosophy of human development shaped by Kierkegaard's idea of life attitudes; and third, the implications and consequences of interpreting a model classical educator who continues to serve as an ideal in our own time. But, fourth, there is one further advantage of exploring Kierkegaard's interpretations of Socrates. It will help us to understand why Kierkegaard disclaims the role of educator. His insistence that "I am not a teacher, only a fellow student," that he was merely turning back upon the age the education that life pressed upon him,[4] will become clearer as we discover that "to be a teacher in the right sense is to be a learner."[5] Eventually Kierkegaard will come to the final position of saying that his entire activity as an author was really his own self-education.[6] Understanding what Kierkegaard means by this self-education is indispensable to an understanding of his idea of authentic individuality. It should also alert us to the problems of reading and interpreting Kierkegaard. By posing simultaneously the situations of both learner and teacher, he brings the dialectic of self-knowledge to a vibrant peak of intensity.

Kierkegaard uses three key infinitives to describe the Socratic postures: to hover, to vanish, and to witness. There are, no doubt, further terms that could be found throughout the authorship, but these seem to be the most vivid and compellingly central ones. He always seems to have Socrates in some kind of motion, corresponding to a key aspect of transformation in a person's life. In his theory of life stages, these infinitives correspond generally to intermediary phases or, if you will, interfacings between spheres of being. We identify them for now as the attitudes of the "ironist," the "humorist," and the ethical-religious individual not yet a Christian whom we might entitle the "theist." These Socratic movements add to the problem of invisibility. But they help to remind us that the correct orientation toward Socrates is one of self-knowledge, that efforts to grasp Socrates' concrete historical reality become moments in which the very assumptions of our approach may become transparent to us. This is also the case for Socrates' pupil Kierkegaard and the many-sidedness of his activity as an educator. We therefore embark upon tracing the journey of the educative thinker, brought from the *agora* of ancient Athens to the nineteenth-century Danish market capital of Copenhagen by means of an allegory of education.

1.
Socrates Hovering:
The Becoming of Subjectivity

Socrates has served for centuries as a model for the educator. The dramatic unfolding of his life and teaching in the *Dialogues* combined with the variety of views which Plato, Aristophanes, and Xenophon gave of him has made possible a wide range of interpretations that were often based upon a so-called authentic understanding of "how it really was with Socrates." Within the humanistic tradition, the Socratic mode has survived a multitude of disagreements and misunderstandings. In the nineteenth century a concerted effort of scholarship aimed to distinguish the Socratic posture and person from what was essentially Platonic doctrine. One of the distinguishing elements was the presence or absence of philosophical "results." The essential Socrates was the ironical gadfly of the marketplace who brought traditional Greek life-views to a standstill through a form of dialectic based upon interrogation—question and answer. A result characteristic of "earlier" *Dialogues* was one terminating in contradiction and incommensurability, proving the undoing of a particular character's self-certainty—Sophist or *rhetor* (politician)—who would represent commonly held views of society, law, education, and knowledge. This undoing of the accepted and often unexamined cultural point of view led to an *aporia:* a theoretical puzzle experienced as doubt. The

Platonic, on the other hand, could be clearly discerned in those *Dialogues* that yielded a doctrine, resolution, theoretical solution, or, generally, a positive result.

The absence of positive ascertainment in the portrayal of Socrates' lifework, and the meaning and implication of the *aporetic* moment, as reported in the earlier *Dialogues*, served Kierkegaard as an interpretive model for the individual who eventually became the "existential" Socrates. While he modeled himself on the Socratic, drawing definite conclusions about this philosophical absence, Kierkegaard passed through several interpretations of this puzzling Socratic vacancy. He placed himself in the space and temporal moment cleared by Socratic action, perceiving the inner limit whose emptiness suggested a shape created by the cunning master of paradoxical self-knowledge. Initially, he apprehended him as the teacher whose primary concern seemed to be personal salvation, and only secondarily the deliverance of others from the pitfalls of ignorance. Gradually, as we shall see, Kierkegaard discovered a greater fecundity implied by this educative shape. In the present section we begin to explore the ironical Socrates, whose speech enables him to hover magically above the scene of a dissolving world view. Later it is Socrates himself who vanishes.

Kierkegaard's first approach to the Socratic posture cannot be understood in historical isolation. His primary contact with the Socratic is already present as an interpretation historically handed down through Hegelian dialectics.

The description advanced by Hegel in his *History of Philosophy* (vol. 1) crystallized what became a dominant conception of Socrates throughout the 1830s and 1840s. Hegel describes as the "mental turning point" in the history of philosophy the announcement by Socrates that the truth of the objective world lay in the thoughts of the subjects who comprehended that world. The thinking subject was Socrates' epoch-making idea. He recognized the treasure that thought could apprehend by reflecting on itself instead of straining into the external world in search of clues. Socrates discovered the freedom of consciousness to think itself and thereby to think the content of thought in the form of universals.

Hegel's Socrates evokes two fundamental movements in the life of self-reflecting subjectivity: first, the "return" to self, which, since the self becomes its own object, limits the self and identifies consciousness as the life of a Person, i.e., as self-consciousness; and, second, having established the subject and "coming out from particular subjectivity," the self reprojects through universal principles its ideas as identical with the objective world.[1] Hence, the discovery of the Person as a self-limiting agent (and therefore infinite) and the identity of that limit with the "truth" of the objective world are first presented in the life of Socrates. Socrates becomes then more a figure of personality (individuality) than a philosopher—a speculating metaphysician.

Socratic teaching centered principally around the awakening of subjectivity in others. His mode of instruction was, according to Hegel, the feigning of ignorance. By calling for assistance in curing his own lack of certain knowledge, Socrates was able to elicit contradictions in the opinions of his fellow citizens. His mode of discourse carried him into collision with the self-certainty of the other. The meeting of ascertained ignorance ("Socratic ignorance") and unexamined opinion produced a subjective dialectic resulting in irony or dissemblance. Socrates exercised this irony as a technique for drawing out the other in order to assist him in self-education. So closely bound to his personal life were these methods that they constituted a way of being a person rather than a system of knowledge or epistemology.[2]

Socrates was skillful enough to enter the assumed world of the other's unreflected consciousness, where ideas dwelled in a state of suspended animation as abstractions. This, and his ability to reveal how those abstractions might be made concrete, might be brought to the life of thought and possibility in the form of ideas, enabled him to bring about development in the mind of the other person. Socratic irony had the great quality of showing how the concreteness of abstract ideas could be developed enabling them, as concepts, to enter the life of consciousness. Hegel could therefore well accredit Socrates as a bearer of the positive progress of thought which succeeding generations of thinkers were to enrich. But his irony, thought Hegel, was best understood as a single moment in the development of subjectivity—a primitive first movement which, by virtue of the reflection it could produce, freed a moral insight from the tangle of a traditional ethic.[3]

As a heuristic device, Socrates' irony functioned as a powerful instrument for dissolving the immediately given natural knowledge constituted by inherited traditional cultural values and heritages which had lost ethical worth in the substantiality of fourth century Athens. Irony set the infinite freedom of the person (subjectivity) over against the customs and laws of the state. The effect of Socratic irony was to uncover an awareness of consciousness' capacity to discover the truth by reflecting upon itself, simultaneously raising into doubt that which it had assumed in immediacy and, negating that knowledge, asserting the freedom of inwardness over the restrictions of the previously established external world. Small wonder that Socrates became identified as a threat, his irony causing his "tragic" downfall. And Hegel himself could see that if one carelessly overlooked the movement that reconnected this truth of subjectivity—these universals—with the objective world, one might come to believe that subjectivity in the form of irony was the highest possible moment of mind and was therefore the highest achievement of the person.

Hegel claimed that the "universal irony of the world" was taken to be just such a highest possibility by the poets and philosophers of the Romantic school. Friedrich von Schlegel and Fichte, to name the most important, raised subjectivity as expressed in the ironic state of mind to the level of divine knowing. Thus, these proponents of the individual's freedom helped to nullify the world by making the person independent of everything. Rather than achieving the heights of knowledge and selfhood, Hegel said, they canceled out everything ultimate and made the depth of life the depth of emptiness.[4] Socratic irony had its value, but this value when isolated could get out of proportion, thought Hegel. The Romantics had misunderstood the Socratic in creating their own form of irony. What sort of teacher then was Socrates?

Socrates was the educator of self-consciousness and played a vital historical role in the development of reason. But, thought Hegel, he was paradoxically not a teacher as is commonly understood since he had nothing to teach anyone that they themselves did not already potentially know. He had no body of knowledge to communicate, unlike the Sophists, but he could be instrumental in awakening the minds of others. Rather than a teacher, he was a seducer who inspired the desire for knowledge by revealing its absence. He sought to make the truly virtuous life a puzzle, the missing pieces of which each person had to discover within himself. Reflection —the search for these pieces—and thinking—assembling them—were inextricable processes indicating that thinking and subjectivity were coeval. The ability to operate with abstract ideas and the inward comprehension of universal principles freed the mind from the illusions of concrete immediacy—in which it had not even discovered its lack of knowledge, its ignorance. This discovery was the necessary process in the formation of the Person.

The action of Socratic irony produced a new possibility in the life of the person. It brought about conscious ignorance, that state of mind that makes knowing possible. The negation of what formerly was grasped in the immediacy of concrete intuition or natural knowledge, raised the question of where positive knowledge would then come from. An uncultured man, like a child, lives in a world of concrete individual ideas. But the individual, said Hegel, who grows and educates himself, "goes back into himself as thinking" and reflects on what is universal in thought, thus establishing the same in permanency. The individual discovers an immutable knowledge immanent within himself. Consciousness is *sur-*

prised by what it finds in consciousness. First it simply knew about things by belief or appearance. Then it discovered, by reflection, that it knew nothing. Suddenly, there opened up a new *way* of knowing which canceled the emptiness of ignorance. The consciousness of not-being with the truth made being with the truth possible.[5] Socrates made an effort to produce a conception of the Good. Irony was the vehicle for carrying out the surprise that could awaken it.

"What they knew refuted itself," said Hegel about the ancient Greeks, "from which the necessity for earnest effort after knowledge is a result."[6] The coming into being of self-conscious reflection arising through doubt and negation parallels the coming into being of the Person as self-conscious subjectivity. The individual makes knowledge "his own" by identifying the "me" and "mine" of thought. Logically, the dialectical process exhibits three stages, which Hegel simply mentions in the discussion of Socrates' method.[7] The potential person (consciousness) has his being in the immediacy of existence, though it is an indeterminate being lacking a true subject or knower. Socrates enters as the propagator of selfhood and stirs up doubt through irony. The individual enters a state of negation, or mediation, of nonbeing as a knower and, in fact, of not-being-a-person. Then, logically, there follows a second reflection, one which may occupy a considerable period of dialogue, in which the universals of being arise as the negation of the former negation. This new possible being (knowing) is not indeterminate like the earlier state, but is rather determinate being or self-consciousness. And this new possibility for being is different also in having become aware of itself as full of potential, as having a project of going-back-into-itself. Hegel called this animation of thinking "becoming."

Becoming is the essential movement of the thinking person. It is the activity of self-conscious reflection in which selfhood is being continually distinguished in the act of appropriating knowledge. Socrates awakened some of his fellow Athenians to consciousness of having the potential of action and knowledge in their thought. The real existence of knowledge as inwardly immanent was a first step in discovering Spirit or Mind within the human realm. Instead of the external substantiality of the Greek gods, suggests Hegel, the Greeks came to have the insight that God takes human form.[8]

We may summarize Hegel's view by saying that Socrates educated his fellow men to the realization that the truth of being was Becoming. The truth of the objective world was located in the reflection of subjectivity. Once having made that discovery they would then automatically make themselves as subjectivity identical with the Good as objectivity. The resulting synthesis would then be the universal and immutable from which morality, the knowledge of right and wrong, could be derived.

Socrates does not produce a doctrine or final morality from this movement of Becoming. Leaving such determinations to the thinking of each person, he fails to carry further the necessity of bringing the freedom of subjectivity into line with choosing the Good. He did not consider that it was possible to know what is right and yet choose what is wrong. Doing wrong, evil, was for him an absence of knowing what is right—nothing more. Hegel is critical of this, and it influences his interpretation of Socrates' ideas about conflict with the State.

Because morality was valid on both sides, Socrates came into collision with the State. Divine rights, natural morality (objective freedom) were put into opposition with the "really divine," consciousness or subjectivity (subjective freedom). Because he was not unaware of the consequences in his assertion of subjective freedom, Socrates became, in Hegel's eyes, a tragic figure sacrificed to the "fruit of the tree of knowledge of good and evil," which became a universal principle of philosophy for all time.[9]

Kierkegaard's first depiction of Socrates agrees with Hegel's on two cardinal points: first, that Socrates' life represents, first and last, the flowering of subjectivity—not speculative philosophy but individual activity; and, second, that Socratic irony introduced the reflective life of self-consciousness—the "return" to self and negation of substantiality in the given cultural view.[10] Was Kierkegaard a Hegelian philosopher in his initial depiction of the ancient wise man? His answer comes in the essay on irony (*Concept of Irony*, 1841), and is itself ironical.

Kierkegaard did not agree with Hegel that Socratic irony was a *method* of subjective dialectics which Socrates used in order to lead men through thought to the true good and to the universal idea. He rejects this systematic form of interpretation which places Socrates as a moment among moments determined by a logic of historical necessity. If we make such an interpretation upon a historical personage we must also make it upon ourselves as thinking subjects. If Socrates' chief standpoint truly was irony, rather than irony serving him for some other purpose, then an interpretation faithful to the phenomena of his life's activity should do justice also to its essence. Since the inner and the outer, the essence and the phenomena, of Socrates' life in irony are different—indeed, opposite—an interpretation would have to assume the nature of this hidden inwardness. Therefore, it is really Socrates who does the interpreting when someone tries to understand him and deliver a meaning to succeeding generations. By aiming to let Socrates' irony, and hence negativity, stand in its own independent light, Kierkegaard took an ironical standpoint toward Hegel's historical logic by bringing it to a standstill through a Hegelian type of interpretation which insisted that no further movement toward positivity could be elicited from the Socratic position. Only by being unfaithful "to the direction of the current in Socrates' life"[11] could such an interpretation as Hegel's be made possible. Not only does Kierkegaard get Socrates to hover in irony but, in so doing, he puts Hegelianism in a state of suspended animation—undone by its own interpretation of the undoer.

Irony, according to Kierkegaard, was the truth of Socrates' life, not a method; in his view the irony of Socrates did not aim at a result, at a concept of the good, but was a *striving* toward the good. Kierkegaard placed emphasis on the activity of Socrates' life in an effort to restore to reality the existence of an individual which had become, with Hegel, reduced to a mere moment in the evolution of a concept. Socrates did not direct his ironic mentality against some particular aspects of Hellenism with which he disagreed: "the whole substantial life of Hellenism had lost its validity for him, that is to say, the established actuality had become unreal to him, not in some particular aspect—but in its totality as such."[12] In its rebellion against the total scope of his environment Socrates' existence was irony. If irony was for him only a method then it would be untrue to say that Socrates had nothing to teach. He could have taught a set of skills by which his friends might have become another group of Sophists. This was not Socrates intention. Kierkegaard has caught Hegel in the act of having to posit a positive result for the life of a world-historical individual. But if the concept is to be true to the phenomena, it would have to be said that the study of Socrates reveals an unassimilable individual whose life manifested the entry of the subject into philosophy.

Like Hegel, Kierkegaard regarded the Socratic moment of truth and the emergence of personality as founded on the "return to self." But Kierkegaard attempted to show that Socrates never wished to resolve the moment of reflection into a result. He maintained himself as pure empty subjectivity in tension with its possession of the absolute as a nothingness. Irony as a determination of personality "seeks back into itself, terminates in itself—except that in this movement irony returns empty-handed."[13] The relation of the person to the world through the ironic attitude is a nonrelation, a "skeptical closedness" (*epoche*). The skepticism here attributed to Socrates is a suspension of judgment in the sense that it is "close-fisted," *paaholden*—a "holding on to" personality in affirmation of an incipient self. Socrates is not an "unhappy consciousness" though the form irony later took with the Romantics became so.

As a world-historical beginning for personality Socrates is positive; but as only a beginning and nothing more, he is a negative moment. "To know that one is ignorant is the beginning of wisdom, but if one knows no more than this, it is only a beginning. It is this knowledge which holds Socrates ironically aloft."[14] Not just a contest of interpretations but a competition of philosophical styles of interpretation is at stake here. Kierkegaard wants to get his Socrates to "hover" just as Socrates, through irony, raised the individual out of immediate existence, emancipating him but thereafter letting him hover as if "suspended between two magnets."[15] These two magnets, attracting and repelling, are apparently allusions to the dialectic of existence—the good and bad, right and wrong, being and nonbeing. In getting his Socrates to hover Kierkegaard frees his interpretation from the imposition of a system and its dialectical requirements. Hovering Socrates stands as the primary moment of the person, as infinite possibility. Kierkegaard is attempting to steal away Hegel's notion of becoming, making Hegel's logic seem static and incapable of accounting for development—the passage of the individual from possibility to actuality. He converts the notion of becoming to his own dialectical purposes.

Kierkegaard conceives Socratic irony, using Hegelian language, as "infinite absolute negativity." Now in Hegelian dialectics, infinite would mean returned to self versus the spurious infinite; absolute would mean completely self-contained; and negativity would render determinate, through mediation as negation of the negation. Infinite absolute negativity is for Hegel the Truth as it is apprehended in self-conscious knowledge. But "infinite absolute negativity" has a subtly different meaning for Kierkegaardian dialectical irony.

> Thus we have irony as infinite absolute negativity. It is negativity because it only negates; it is infinite because it negates not this or that phenomenon; and it is absolute because it negates by virtue of a higher which is not. Irony establishes nothing, for that which is to be established lies behind it.[16]

What is the concept of Truth for Hegel is for Kierkegaard the condition of irony characterizing the emergence of individuality. By implication, then, philosophy cannot abrogate (*aufheben*) and preserve the Socratic, just as Socrates did not provide a positive result. There is no "after Socrates"—philosophically speaking—since, in effect, every emergence of individuality is contemporary with Socrates. To go beyond Socrates is, for Kierkegaard, to go beyond philosophy into religious life.

Irony is an act that determines the self over against the nothingness of the world. Irony is an attitude in which the ironist finds himself, as determinate being (*dasein*), related to the absolute given in the form of nothingness. The person, as ironist, emerges as the formal abstract synthesis—the mere "outline" of personality—in subjectivity: the interpenetration of finite existence with the infinite freedom of possibility. The form of the self has emerged, its content is a matter of the future. The ironic self has no-thingness, its actuality lies between the temporal present or existential presence to self and the possibilities of what it could become in the future, its own future. As such the ironic self is what it is not-yet, and is not-yet what it is. As a determination of selfhood, irony causes the contradiction of the finite and the infinite dwelling together to come into being.

Irony, considered as Kierkegaard's version of Socrates, is then a dwelling-within-contradiction by the person, rather than a method of advancing to the resolution of the Idea of the good, by the abstract thinking of the individual.

The Socratic posture becomes more concrete with Kierkegaard when focus is placed upon the educator's irony in relationship to his students. One has only to look for reference to Alcibiades to find the right context of the Socratic education. Whether we look in the thesis chapter on "The Conception Made Possible," or in the one where the conception (i.e., of irony) is "Made Actual," the description is the same with regard to educator Socrates.

Did he communicate directly to fulfill or enrich his pupil

Alcibiades? Was there a profitable exchange of ideas, a rich outpouring on one side and a grateful reception on the other? No, says Kierkegaard, for then the love between Socrates and his pupil would have culminated in a common object or moment of infinite synthesis wherein they would have become joined to the Idea. What third element, what Idea, is it that would have united them? Kierkegaard does not make this clear but uses the Hegelian term, "the Idea," in each instance. Here, however, we grasp the implication by virtue of the situation in which it is employed.[17] Eros, Kierkegaard reminds us, is born of poverty and plenty (*poros* and *penia*) and, as their son, embodies a duality. Socrates arouses the soul of Alcibiades who is infatuated by his intellectual possibilities. Alcibiades, however, cannot rid himself of the desire to possess the Socratic personality. There is desire on both sides: Socrates for the higher, Alcibiades for the lower nature. If these two were to become united, their union would represent an identity—which is what Alcibiades apparently seeks, but which Socrates' irony prevents. The Idea is then the possession of identity, Socrates and Alcibiades united in the positive Idea of love. But such an act would mean an injustice to the god Eros and the duality of love. Instead, there remains a "passionate turmoil" between Socrates and his pupil. Through his irony Socrates loosens the ties of prejudice and frees his pupils from intellectual rigidity. His questions help to prepare for the moment of transformation. In the twinkling of an eye everything is changed and the world of consciousness becomes illuminated for his students. Meanwhile, Socrates, the ironic observer, stands aside watching them in their surprise. Does his irony then free the pupils for the surprise of consciousness, or does it make them dependent upon him and his personality as in the case of Alcibiades? Kierkegaard seems a little unclear about the consequences of the Socratic posture.

Socrates seemed to take a great interest in the youth. His questioning and inquiring flattered them and assisted their discovery of a new outlook. Just when they might have expected something more from Socrates, some explanation of what they had come to see, he left them in silence. He had been the lover—initiating the erotic dialectic of communication—but he became the beloved. What the pupils sought they identified with Socrates, but the relationship had already reached its consummation and Socrates gave no more. They pursued him like disciples, but he repulsed them —he the beloved, the recipient through an inversion of the communication. Kierkegaard also states that some pupils became grateful the more they recognized that they were not indebted to Socrates for the treasures of consciousness. Yet, here we have them as pursuing lovers who desired to possess the noble rogue. Should we understand that irony, like Eros, is born of duality; that the individual whose stance is ultimately irony both invites to and evicts from the precinct of his personality?

Socrates was forbidding in his irony. Disguised, mysterious, he initiated "telegraphic communications" which could only be understood at a distance. Yet his messages were seductively inviting. He aimed to set free and left Alcibiades and the others hovering. He aimed to assist their autonomy by insisting upon his own: for him "know thyself" meant, says Kierkegaard, "separate thyself."[18] But a kind of dependency seemed to persist. The ironist opens himself to his Alcibiades, but in the next moment Alcibiades is lost in his power. The communicative event which the Socratic posture helps to create consists in attractions and repulsions. Love and irony go hand in hand, for Socrates' irony stirs up desire, but keeps the would-be possessor in abeyance.

"Irony is the negative in love, the incitement of love," rather than the abiding participation in a fullness.[19] Clearly, Kierkegaard has another kind of love in mind when he makes this distinction—the Christian love or *agape*. It is desire and longing that are called up by Socrates' negative love. Even here, for Kierkegaard, Socratic irony in love is negative. And Socrates, as educator, is seen once more to be hovering, but this time hovering above his would-be lovers who seek and

yet fear to seek indentity with the Socratic personality. We
are left with this ambiguity concerning Socrates and Kierkegaard's interpretation of his posture. Let us summarize this
with Kierkegaard's own words.

> He brought the individual under the force of the dialecti-
> cal vacuum pump, deprived him of the atmospheric air
> in which he was accustomed to breathe, and abandoned
> him. For such individuals everything was now lost,
> except insofar as they were able to breathe in an ether.
> Yet Socrates no longer concerned himself with them, but
> hastened on to new experiments.[20]

Not only Socrates but Kierkegaard too hastens on to new
experiments with irony. His preliminary confrontation with
Socrates uncovers the ambiguous role of the educator's
irony, that is, whether it fosters greater dependency or autonomy. In one sense Kierkegaard's criticism of Socrates that his
ignorance is also a limitation, follows Hegel. But Kierkegaard
begins to see a virtue in this limitedness itself, whereas Hegel
sees it as a vehicle of history. A second implicit criticism is
directed toward the Socratic character whose first love,
philosophy, separates him from his fellow creatures. Is the
intellectual surgery that Socrates performs, his cauterizing
irony, the utmost concern that one individual can show
another? Apparently Socrates receives no further messages
from his daemon who would warn him from the wrong
course of action. His main task is to awaken this inner voice,
this inner teacher, in the minds of the youthful followers. The
chaste and unpossessable beloved of the romantic imagination is further undermined by this conception of the Socratic
posture. Not only does eros signify an impossible union with
the other but, here, it signifies an impossible union with oneself. The residual emotion of the unfulfilled romantic eros
catapults the individual into the infinite, but Kierkegaard's
Socrates can only hover in negativity.

2.
Socrates Vanishing:
The Passion of Subjectivity

Kierkegaard's earliest interpretation of the Socratic figure, under the influence of Hegel, but simultaneously struggling to liberate Socratic action, focuses essentially upon the releasing of subjectivity for which irony clears a space. Emphasis is primarily upon the initial inception of selfhood rather than upon its growth and development. Socrates is foremost a helper who helps himself, who "separates himself" in faithfulness to his own inner voice—his daemon. The maieutic Socrates, or the helper who practices a devotion in reciprocal relationship to others, is not yet born. Kierkegaard is prepared to see a different, an "existential" Socrates, within the Hegelian perspective, but he is not prepared to see beyond the Hegelian except insofar as he introduces an absolute breach of continuity between Socrates and another great teacher in the person of Jesus—the latter representing the positivity or fullness of love.

Three years after the thesis on irony, Kierkegaard wrote and published the *Philosophical Fragments* (1844). There, in that work, Socrates is again a primary figure and represents the "highest relationship that one human being can sustain to another."[1] This relationship sharply divides the humanistic sphere from the relationship distinguishing the religious sphere, namely, between man and God. The life and teaching

of another servant, Christ, is contradistinguished to that of
Socrates. But clearly, if these two teachers can be differenti-
ated it must be because of a fundamental similarity that
allows comparison. Kierkegaard, reflecting through his
pseudonym, Johannes Climacus, raises this comparison in
order to show an absolute separation between Socrates who
is only an "occasion" for another's discovery of the "unknown," and Christ who is the bringer of the very condition
itself for experiencing the positive "unknown"—the Divine.
The entire comparison revolves around the problematic expression, "a historical point of departure," and whether such
a point of departure could ever be sufficient or necessary in
reaching an "eternal consciousness" or "eternal happiness."
The most Socrates can do in these circumstances is to make
an accidental contribution. Christ, on the other hand, is able
to create the moment itself. The unspoken connection between these two figures is implied by the fact that Johannes
Climacus does not postulate two independent kingdoms but,
rather, two different kinds of relationships existing concurrently. Man is the common element in both relationships.
Could it be then that there is something of the Divine in man,
and particularly that there is something of the Divine in Socrates? Is Socrates' life—as a model for the humanistic sphere
—an analogy to Christ's life and the religious sphere? To
speak in such terms would indeed be considered heretical.
Kierkegaard was wise to choose the name of a sixth century
saint as a nominative for this undertaking. His choice was
not arbitrary for he has no other in mind than the author of
the manuscript, *The Ladder of Divine Ascent*. In the following section we journey with Socrates in his rise toward the
positive relationship. Socrates, who though is only an occasion, a "vanishing moment,"[2] is, nevertheless, a notable participant who enables the point of departure signifying an
advance in human development and human consciousness.

By contrast, the portrait of Socrates in *Concept of Irony*
was a still life exhibiting certain Socratic principles. The Socrates of *Philosophical Fragments* and the subsequent *Post-*

script (1846) to the *Fragments* is presented as an authentic human being of flesh and blood, of feeling and insight—not a historical principle but a living reality. If we look, for example, at the Socratic eros of *Concept of Irony* we find a "mere" longing after and striving involved. The duality of the god Eros, poverty and plenty, holds Socrates at a zero point. As a teacher he inspires but is himself immovable, neither advancing nor retreating, neither ascending nor descending, but just hovering beginningly. His position is still in irony when Kierkegaard, in the *Fragments*, speaks of Socratic ignorance as an expression for "his love of the learner, and for his sense of equality with him."[3] It is as if Kierkegaard, like Plato, turned the pejorative meaning of the word *eiron*—which in earlier Greek drama meant imposter, buffoon—inside out to disclose a positive hidden inwardness.[4] Kierkegaard begins to discover something more behind the mask of this buffoon, begins to discover something other than a hovering teacher and master deceiver. Irony, formerly understood as love's undoing, masked by ignorance, now comes forth as "revealed existence" in and through which life is made whole. Love (eros) is a continual striving which expresses "the existence of the subjective thinker." If we shall come to the moment in which Socrates vanishes by virtue of his love of the learner, we will need to understand that what preceeds his disappearance is a passionate prelude. For it is passion that the Socratic eros becomes, the passion of a subjective thinker.

For some philosphies thought begins through doubt or the suspension of given attitudes and assumptions. Kierkegaard translates doubt into the personal, individual sphere where it shows its unified form in irony. What irony accomplishes once and forever with Socrates is the destruction of the natural attitude through indirect means. The person discovers himself while loosing the certainty of objective knowledge. The individual realizes himself as a creature who strives for knowledge. Rather than ask *what* knowledge is, Kierkegaard dwells upon the question of *how* the person stands related to his knowledge. For Kierkegaard Socrates drives a wedge separating knower and known. How one is a knower becomes the foundation for what is known. For what can be known abstractly, Kierkegaard relies upon Hegel's comprehensive enterprise. But faced with the mystery of how any actual person could really come to know with such encompassing completeness, Kierkegaard draws attention to the subject as existing thinker, i.e., as one who does not shed his temporal part in order to grasp the eternal truths, but who is simultaneously a temporal being dialectically related to the timeless.

The emblem of the existing thinker is Socrates the ironist who hovers between experience in the aesthetic mode (sensuous immediacy) and the metaphysical thinker's speculative position. While presenting himself in the personal style of irony which appropriately expresses his "ignorance" and uncertainty, the hovering Socrates reveals the situation and condition of a subjective thinker. His is no longer a "mere" ignorance but a dynamic unknowing serving as foundation for the development of human knowledge, particularly with respect to questions of human happiness and virtue.

Kierkegaard considered the first "historical Socrates" as a symbol of independent being—the separating out of a historical reality from other realities. His reinterpretation makes Socrates a figure of liberation with positive intent. Hegel understands transition as mediation in the dialectical logic; Kierkegaard replaces that with Socratic doubt expressed as irony. For him Socrates represents the moment of dilemma, contradiction, uncertainty, and paradox, when the individual being exists concretely between possibility and actuality, thinking and action, knowledge of the good and good deeds. His is also an inclusive dialectic but one in which the individual dwells within or participates in the contradictions that are the truth of his being. "Reality or existence is the dialectical moment in a trilogy, whose beginning and end cannot be for the existing individual, since *qua* existing individual he is himself in the dialectical moment."[5]

What kind of personal activity does being "in the dialectical moment" indicate? It means that reflection brings the experience of contradiction rather than the idea of mediation. And why do we have the experience of contradiction rather than a gradual transition of levels? Because we take interest in our lives and strive to make manifest the qualitative difference separating what we know we are as empirical egos from what we think, feel, desire, and imagine we would be ideally. And where does this ideal imperative come from? It arises in human passion. What is passion? Passion is the endurance of suffering; and to suffer means to experience change in modality of being while remaining unchanged in essence.[6]

Kierkegaard refers us to Aristotle's concept of movement (*kinesis*) as meaning "to suffer change." Suffering change in the way of being is certainly a process of becoming for what was not-being (*dynamis*). Passion therefore is the quality of striving to come into being; it is the process of becoming. The kind of change involved, which is a suffering, is temporal, and the ideal striven for is imagined as infinite—that is, perfect and completed.

Passion arising through imagination projects the ideal which is infinite, complete in itself, autonomous. But the individual who begins to strive after that ideal experiences the gravity of passion which accentuates the condition of empirical existence—human finitude. Finding the image of the infinite within the scope of his intimate possibility, the individual simultaneously becomes conscious of his being penetrated by finite existence. Is there a way in which he could overcome finitude? Perhaps the individual could think through existence and transform it into the form of an immutable idea. Let us say the individual thinks passionately about existence; what does he discover? He experiences "becoming infinite;" he realizes himself as both becoming and ideal being. He suffers the process of becoming the infinite ideal and dwells in the moment of the paradox. The passion of the existing subject renders him infinite in the eternity that imagination has represented to him. Yet, he is at the same time most definitely himself.[7]

For such a moment to be anything more than a "fantastic rendezvous in the clouds" requires that the individual risk the self-certainty of the empirical ego by choosing the uncertainty of the possible with his full being. The individual gives up certainty—albeit, that of a conditioned self—for the position of ignorance with regard to the truth of the immutable. Choosing to be the truth that is contradiction means a willingness to become paradoxical. For when what is apparently a contradiction is seen to hold an unexpected truth, the surprise to consciousness calls forth an "appropriation process" founded on the truth of existence, on subjectivity. The paradox, when made personal, points the way through to a deeper dimension while the contradiction still stands as a logical doubt that has taken on new meaning. The contradiction cannot be resolved, but the paradox can be lived through.[8] It is Socrates' merit to have discovered the paradoxical position of the subjective thinker: the truth of the immutable is only comprehensible if the empirical ego suspends its knowledge content and, purified by ignorance, strives passionately to embrace the contradiction of existence. How Socrates proceeds to embrace this contradiction relates in a twofold way to the Socratic eros: for one, it is the eternal, and for the other, it is the pupil—the emerging self, which stands for the beloved—as we shall soon see.

Socrates took the problem rather than its solution as the way to wisdom. From Kierkegaard's point of view this amounts to saying that the truth is not a "thing" but a stance in relation to the world—a life posture. If, as Kierkegaard has become famous for saying, "truth is subjectivity," it is so only insofar as the subject brings so much passion together with his thought that the synthesis will be an actual event rather than an experiment in thought. In his second interpretation of Socrates, passion first and last is what Socrates' life symbolizes for Kierkegaard. Without passion there is no movement for the existing thinker. Passion is the affirming motive of development, the willingness to undergo and hence suffer the change of becoming. Passion raises the question of what it is that moves one; of what is to be considered as itself unmoving but moving the self through its developmental actions.

The paradox of subjectivity is that when considered from an experiential point of view the radical orientation of a self-referent being turns an inward movement, an appropriation process, into an outward or upward one in which it gives itself over to what it would have taken possession of in thought. This implies that the concept of truth as subjectivity is itself an ironical truth, as we shall now explore.

The relation of a thinking subject who exists in reflective consciousness—motivated by passion and in the process of becoming—to the unchanging, immutable truth is a contradiction. On one side, from which we begin with Socrates, passion and becoming are the truths of the existing subject. On the other side, imagined and posited by the concept of passionate striving, is the truth of the immutable. Separating the two dimensions is the limitation and also foundation of selfhood—which is temporal existence. Irony, as the originating reflection of the personal activity of development, separates the person from immediacy of self in the aesthetic domain and introduces the new possibility of being which is one of becoming subjective. The timeless or immutable truth is then not the possession of the eternal but the becoming of one's search for immortality. And here is the paradox that an interpretation of Socratic irony may be shown to yield. Kierkegaard explores to the fullest extent the paradox that the irony of subjectivity yields, when he investigates Socrates' relationship to knowledge of the eternal according to the Greek doctrine of recollection (*anamnesis*). For the moment, as a prelude and as a way to make the foregoing clearer, consider the example of the distinction between body and soul.

We find in several *Dialogues* the notion that the soul—which is in possession of timeless truths and eternal knowledge—is contained, trapped, or imprisoned in the body (cf. *Gorgias* 493a). Only by freeing itself of the bodily, mundane life that has caused forgetfulness can the eternal truth be known—or, in this instance, remembered. Put in psychological terms we could say that the body means the conditioned self and the soul indicates the authentic emerging self, the un-conditioned, the self-ideal. It is not strange then that Socrates should often associate the idea of death with this act of remembrance, since only by losing or abandoning the conditioned self, which is a kind of passing away, could the authentic unconditioned self be gained or recollected. Re-birth, in this instance, would mean a re-acquiring of the primordial self. One would then "die" into the immortal self or the timeless truth of being. How one should undertake this process answers the question: What is the body in the body/soul dichotomy? We have answered the question already by calling it conditioning. Socrates does not give quite such a psychological answer.

The body is life experienced as sensation and perception, the world of appearances. Understood in a more existential light, it is the temporal dwelling of a changing and develop-ing being which seeks to be self-integrated or unified with the pure possibilities of its immortal soul—the divine part. One reading of the idea of liberation from the bodily would imply a denial of all that is earthly and temporal. Thinking could be the means by which one recollected the pure immutable-eter-nal truth. Does Socrates stand for this shedding and denial of the bodily, the temporal? Or does his irony suggest the para-doxical thought that human beings have the power to unify the body and soul, the changing and the unchanging, or the conditioned and the unconditioned self? This idea in itself would be ironical since it is the expression of a paradox. But it is so when the individual wills to unite the bodily with the immaterial essence of an individual. The will to bring the temporal sensuous existence into accordance with the time-less, pure being is the passionate striving. The way of pas-sionate striving for the unity of being in time is paradoxical but faithful to the whole truth of human becoming. And it is this wholeness toward which the process moves. The immortality to be discovered is related to present life and the pursuit is guided by actions directed toward the good. And what is the good? The good is the order in all things, including souls, by which they fulfill their place in nature. Immortality then comes to mean a way of acting, of fulfilling an inherent order. And how do we come to know what that order is that should be fulfilled? Here Socrates greets us with his ironical smile. Do we really not know? As an existing knower the individual is not yet in final possession of unchanging truth, but he is on the way to making it conformable to his truth of existence by making himself in existence harmonious with unchanging truth.

Let us recapitulate how the phrase "truth is subjectivity" unites through irony the subjective thinker with his passion. The truth of existence, of person (Y), is a condition of contingency in relation to the nature of immutable truth (X), synthesis with which is anticipated in imagination. The knower becomes sure that for something to be true to his existential situation—the only kind of truth he can be "sure" about—it must be appropriated and made his own. But he becomes further aware that experienced immutable truth (X) will have an effect or alter his condition as existing thinker. Essentially he will remain the same, but existentially his mode of being in relation to the unchanging condition of the truth will be different.

Ironically, at first appearance, the truth to be appropriated is grasped imaginatively as an independent influencing power which is over against the individual's power of existence— ironically, we say, because the thinker has himself posited the independence of a higher power of truth. It is as though apprehended immutable truth (X) served as an exponential factor to the truth of his being an existent entity. Hence, we would have Y raised to the power of X, or Y^X. This is what is meant in saying that the statement "truth is subjectivity" is ironical since it leads to the theology of Augustine or Anselm. Subjectivity posits a power that it itself needs in order to be the synthesis made by conformity of truth of existence to truth of immutability. A higher "outside" power is creatively posited by subjectivity, which renders itself limited and further defined. Each moment of striving for this unity results in a deepening of existential condition, a dimension deepened through the activity of becoming related to eternal truth.

Irony leads to a paradox: motivated by passion, the subject increasingly discovers his limitations for grasping the eternal truth, and that discovery reveals to him more about the powerful nature of the immutable, unconditionec truth.[9] The intensifying of subjectivity is an intensifying of passion, of willingness to suffer change, and as such it displays a willingness to put oneself in the service of the power of the eternal. Taking the liberty to alter Anselm's famous dictum, the ontological argument for the existence of God, we may say that the intensifying of subjectivity depends on "that greater than which I cannot think and without which I as subject cannot be thought to be an existing individual."

As subjectivity increasingly discovers the truth of its inwardness, it realizes its dependency upon the higher power that is felt as objectively independent of itself though posited from within its own being. Eventually that eternal objectivity appears to be the controlling factor in the relation of the contingent to the immutable (Y to X). And it comes to be understood that while the contingent (Y) posits the immutable (X), the immutable is the first condition of the contingent's (Y's) act of positing the immutable (X) in the first place: hence, creation human and creation divine. The self needs the higher power to rest unified in itself as the fulfillment of its passionately projected possibility. Kierkegaard summarizes this himself in his formula for the realized self in the opening pages of *The Sickness unto Death:* "by relating itself to its own self and by willing to be itself, the self is grounded transparently in the power which posited it."[10]

We return to the Socratic eros by way of the passionate striving of the subjective thinker. We remarked earlier that Socrates demonstrated a twofold relationship in directing his energies toward the eternal unknown, attempting to embrace the contradictory aspects of being, the finite and the infinite. In remembering the preexistent soul, Socrates practiced a self-remembrance through which he paid attention not only to the eternal truth but also to those who sought after that truth—the learner, his pupil.

Aristotle, in his *Ethics* (1126b, 6. 1127b), points to the man of virtue as a middle station, a mean, between the ironist (mock-modest) and imposter (boastful) types of character.[11] If this middle figure also possessed passion, says Aristotle, he would resemble a friend, since the friend tolerates and resents the right things for the right reasons, i.e., his is a trustworthy affection. But for Aristotle the man of virtue has his sights set upon moral goodness over and above the feelings of human relationships. Kierkegaard seems to have moved the ironist toward this median position and given him a degree of fellow feeling. The Socratic *eros* becomes transformed into something closer to a Socratic *philos*, friendship. This becomes clearer when we examine Kierkegaard's understanding of how Socrates practiced his theory of recollection.

The idea that knowledge is found in recollection expresses the deepest intuition of Greek philosophy. In postulating the soul as prior to the body, an original state of being and knowledge is assumed to lie outside of time and the existent order. Self-knowledge, which is the basis for all other forms of knowing, empirical as well as transcendent, necessitates a process of remembering or re-collecting the eternity that lies prior to corporeal being. By shedding his temporal condition man could theoretically return to this original state and make actual this immanent truth that is his eternal possession. Socrates pronounces this doctrine on a number of occasions (*Meno, Phaedo*) in order to initiate a certain kind of action in the mind of the other. Kierkegaard and his pseudonyms can be a little confusing about the Socratic relationship to the theory of recollection. In *Concept of Irony* he says that Socrates' relationship to the doctrine is, as we might expect, ironical. In the *Philosophical Fragments* he suggests that Socrates is really promoting the theory of *anamnesis*. And in the

Postscript he asserts again that Socrates' attitude is one of irony. A footnote in the *Postscript* to a section recapitulating the argument of the *Fragments* explains that in that work Socrates was allowed to stand for the doctrine of recollection for the purpose of simplifying the dialectic between the Greek (pagan) and the Christian consciousness.

The Kierkegaardian Socrates of *Concept of Irony* uses the doctrine of recollection ironically or negatively, in distinction to Plato who gives it a positive result. Recollection is the process of following the "retrograde development" of self back to eternity, and in this sense "in opposition to the movement of life" which is temporally forward. According to the Platonic mode, mankind comes into the world with an abundance of human endowment. But Socratically, having gotten the whole of actuality disaffirmed through irony, he "refers mankind to a recollection that recedes further and further toward a past which is itself receding as far back in time as the origin of that noble family which no one can remember."[12]

Socratic recollection achieves two results or has a twofold significance. First, it suggests that the way to eternal (immutable) knowledge consists in following back *one's own* self-history in inward contemplation rather than mistaking the eternal for something objective and external. The theory of recollection makes the individual knower "essentially *integer*," unified through inwardness by means of initiation into the mysterious formula "truth is subjectivity" ("truth lies in the inner man"). And this is prerequisite to the journey through existence, which, second, gains decisive significance because, though at any moment its negation is immanent by virtue of the possibility of taking oneself back into eternity, the likelihood of recollecting eternity collides with the paradox that the process utilizes time to take place.[13] The outcome is comic pathos. The individual existent in time is himself the promise of eternity, but he needs time to make the journey back to origin. The promise is also the paradox.

Between the Thesis on irony and the *Postscript* Socrates'

relating of the doctrine of recollection becomes a rite of initiation—the inauguration of the subjective thinker. Whereas in the Thesis recollection leads to a negative result, the negation of development and history, by the time of the *Postscript* it is seen to embody a positive consequence authenticating the unity of the subject and his personal history however paradoxical that history is shown to be.

In the *Fragments,* where Socrates is made to represent the doctrine of recollection, emphasis is placed upon the dialectic between the Greeks's ("Paganism's") conception of a preextent eternality (recollection) and Christianity's future ideal (the "moment"). Kierkegaard evokes the concept of the Christian cosmology of time. For our present purposes we focus upon the treatment given there of the Socratic educator who is still held up as an ideal within the humanistic domain.

We have already mentioned that in the *Fragments* Socrates' ignorance has become an expression for "his love of the learner." We further note that Socrates has risen to such a station in life that as a paradigm of the teacher his way can be compared to that of Christ as a teacher. Socrates' teaching is radically different from the teaching of Christ since Christ is no mere occasion but a creator of occasions—the bringer of Truth. But Socrates is at least comparable on all points. What of Christ's love for mankind and the understanding which that act of giving requires? Without a common understanding, the learner and teacher are not equals. If they cannot reach an equality that would allow a true meeting in time then the teacher appears either too high or too low for the learner. By taking the form of the humblest, the servant, Christ is able to unite himself with mankind. He gives his love and is no deceiver.

Since Socrates is not a god but one whose life circumstances help to make him a teacher, the learner ought not to seek union with a Socratic teacher nor should that teacher allow the deception to operate that the learner owes him anything. Christ is not an ironist because his servant form is commensurate with his teaching, service, and love of mankind. A king who would marry a humble maiden could appear in a beggar's cloak in order not to humiliate his beloved and to ascertain that her love is truly for him, the man, rather than in obedience to the power of a king. But he would know that he deceives her by his disguise since he really is a king. He could show himself to the maiden in all his pomp and power so that the maiden forgets herself in worshipful admiration. But, alas, he cannot be satisfied with a deception that destroys the very soul he seeks to glorify. The king can never reach a common understanding with his beloved, since his position rules out such an understanding, and therefore such a king is indeed a tragic figure. Between the worldly king and the divine Christ is Socrates the teacher.

Socrates also needs the reciprocal understanding that his love for the learner is truly a love of that which is eternal, divine in the learner, and that this love is precisely a celebration of the mutual mystery of a highest Unknown which exists in each soul. But, alas, Socrates would be turned into a deceiver since his disciples cannot understand this equality but, instead, attribute the higher power to Socrates rather than seeing it in themselves. In order to do justice to them and to himself Socrates takes to the offensive, to irony. He purposely deceives them into thinking that he is empty and barren of knowledge rather than having them delude themselves into thinking of the simple wise man as something that he was not, that is, a divine benefactor. But in this case his deception is truthful to the situation, that all are equidistant from the eternal. Hence, his ignorance, though like the king's beggarly cloak, hides and reveals him so that his irony is true for what is left unsaid and is faithful to that which is said.

Kierkegaard remarks that Socrates is equally autopathic and sympathetic.[14] He is as much for himself as for the other. His life and its circumstances constitute an occasion for him to become a teacher. He in turn gives occasion for others to learn something. Do they learn something *from* him? No, the relationship between teacher and learner is rather that each becomes the occasion for the other to understand himself.

And here is the mutuality that cannot exist between king and maiden, between the higher and the lower, because their respective situations precisely prevent such reciprocal understanding. But does Socrates or his pupil come to understand the other? Here, once again, we reach a silence. The learner and the teacher are united by virtue of a common enterprise that is announced through the theory of recollection. Each turns inward toward the preexistent or, at least, immanent Unknown. They do not turn back outward toward each other but instead the occasioned and the occasioner vanish into the moment of recollected eternity. The mutuality involving teacher and learner, that each becomes the occasion for the other's entrance into the process, and that an equality of unknowing relates them as lovers of that which is absent— the desire for the not-yet, the invisible—is all that remains of the Socratic midwifery. Like a strong drug whose ingestion becomes a lost instant in the eternity of the inward journey, Socrates disappears the moment the learner is "reminded" that he is himself a center of knowledge.

Socrates no longer hovers because his life is bound to the life of the learner in reciprocal assistance. His negativity discloses a positive sympathy. The deeper inwardness of his motive reveals a higher ideal, which he must preserve and protect, but which he is able to share with the learner to the very threshold of the vanishing moment. Socrates is neither prophet nor tragic hero. The prophet envisages and intimates a turning point; tragic heroes fight for it; though related as heroes are to the god Eros (*Cratylus* 398d), Socrates embodies a comic pathos. Socrates "has advanced beyond the reach of his age and opened a front against it. That which shall come is hidden from him, concealed behind his back, but the actuality he hostilely opposes is the one he shall destroy."[15] Through the theory of recollection Socrates orients the learner to the Unknown of his own inner life. And though it may seem preexistent, since time is required for its appropriation it could comically be said of Socrates that he walks backward into the future.

Kierkegaard, through his Socrates, attempts to "hollow out the kernel" of speculative metaphysics by refuting either feature of a systematic philosophy: determinism or immanence. He makes it clear that all metaphysical systems that presuppose a prior unconditioned state, an original fullness, and seek passage through thought back to a pristine unity by emptying time itself, will only founder on the paradox of existence: the one element that cannot be abrogated is the temporal. The doctrine of recollection provides Kierkegaard with an image of speculation: a taking oneself back through time and through history as the content of time, back through memory to an unparadoxical eternity the possession of which amounts to a form of self-redemption and quest of the rational over existence. However possible such a journey of self might be for Socrates and his cohorts, the voyage of discovery would mean the promotion of a paradoxical accomplishment—that one attains a remembrance of the eternal by simultaneously forgetting oneself.

Kierkegaard's Socrates presents the recollective process in a comical light. The whole process becomes ridiculous when we are reminded that the temporal dimension simply cannot be shed except at the expense of one's humanity. Like the dancer who in leaping thinks that he actually could fly and consequently falls on his face, eternity in the doctrine of recollection becomes similarly comical. It is Socrates who is made to appear the new buffoon; he proposes the leap, but disdains the fall. He introduces the eternal knowledge that is trapped in the body—in forgetfulness. He identifies the unknown while simultaneously putting it almost completely out of play. The preexistent eternality of the soul can no longer be reached, but we go on trying for it and, with the correct reflection, we discover how absurd our own efforts really are. Nevertheless, in the effort—though comical—of striving to reach an inward eternal truth of self, the individual does unite himself in action, becoming the singular being whose life is a journey to an unknown place, itself receding like the shadow of the one who walks after it. Only a miracle could enable the individual to reach his goal, immortal as he may be. Such a miracle Kierkegaard introduces with the Christ teacher—which is a story we cannot hope to adequately enter upon here. Before the Christ teacher makes his appearance, however, the Socratic teacher disappears. This is Socrates' second comical act, to vanish at the moment of birth. But why should he remain? His work is done, the eternal unknown has been identified, the pupil has embarked upon a journey, or, consistent with the maieutic metaphor, has gotten pregnant with the idea, an idea that is only an impetus to becoming oneself. Socrates is free of the burden of eros. He does not implant the idea in the mind of the other, he merely assists in its deliverance. Eros in the erotic sense becomes philos in the sense of friendship. Though there is mutual stimulation, mutual occasioning, Socrates does not create a community of followers, because each one is isolated in his own process. Since this is not the final Socratic interpretation, the final posture of an ethical educator, there may be a further advance. But we notice a significant change in the Socratic irony as it now relates to recollecting oneself.

Knowledge = recollection was the equation of speculative metaphysics. But the process of recollection leads to a paradox of the finite process having an infinite goal. The expression of this paradox is Socratic irony. Yet, as Socrates becomes more positive for Kierkegaard, we see that this irony discloses an even higher human truth: the knowledge of what it means to exist. Irony = knowledge. But when a wistful gesture points to something lesser, irony becomes a kind of melancholic sigh, a sigh of resignation. When irony points wistfully toward that which is greater than itself, though out of reach, it becomes something quite different; it becomes humor. And when Socrates and the Socratic occasion becomes a vanishing act, he plays the part of a humorist like the pseudonymous Johannes Climacus—"an existing humoristic psychologist"—who is his author.[16]

His ignorance as love for the learner signifies the transformed Socratic helper. What for Hegel is a dialectical strat-

egy, and that which appears to Kierkegaard as a life-form
first cold, critical, and repelling—later understood as an expression of a passionate subjective thinker's confrontation
with the paradoxical—becomes an expression for the depth
dimension in Socrates' life by means of which he opens the
possibility of a shared situation in striving toward truth of
being. The Socratic ignorance is no longer a mere stopping
point in which the helper hovers above the scene. Nor is the
Socratic ignorance a guise for the irony whose apparent earnestness really discloses the jest that brings a dialogue to
silence and to an end without result. The Socratic ignorance,
within the interpretation of Kierkegaard's maturer view, expresses a form of intercourse that unites through sympathy
the needful becoming of each participant and serves to discover a common situation out from which new life may be
born.

The Socratic helper is a humorist. Was he not an ironist?
Yes, he is also an ironist. The humorist lets the jest convey a
deeper seriousness, the ironist's seriousness disguises his critical wit. The rejoinder of an ironist serves to prevent a conversation from becoming a true conversation while giving the
appearance of such an interchange. The ironist hovers about
the scene of a dialogue, all the while asserting his self-assur-
ance, his autonomy as pure subjectivity. But the humorist
advances an awareness of human development through the
wistful expression of what it means for him to exist as one
who dwells in the contradictions of life, who experiences the
despair that comes with the suffering passion of transformation. The humorist, ethical educator Socrates, jestingly
reveals in his utterances the limits of human striving. His expressive life provides an invitation to dialogue through
assuming the situation of difficulty on the part of the other.
The humorist's rejoinder, rather than saying something less
(irony), says something more through the profound seriousness that lies beneath the jest.[17]

The humorist has his jest out front and the scope of his
humor represents the highest and most inclusive form for the

comical. The comical, as with irony, often makes the other its victim, often establishes a comparison between the better and the worse in human character. But humor is comprehensive and embraces the other by first letting go of itself. Humor then requires the humility that lets something more be seen, as if in an instant the humorist's release of authority, his personal letting-go in positive ignorance, in short, his wistful receptivity to something higher, is experienced as an encompassing moment of totality.

Does the immediate and encompassing effect of humor make it a direct form of communication? It may seem that the humorist is speaking directly. But it is more correct to understand that when the humorist speaks, the listener does not get a direct communication, "but is set into motion."[18] But why should the humorist need to announce his serious side with jesting? If what a person wishes to say is so inward, so spiritually comprehensive a life content, that every direct form is unsatisfactory, incommensurable, especially where the life experience involves great contradictions whose sting is felt, then an indirect form of discourse is required.[19]

The individual's authority to be a fool in a world of his own making signifies the mood that underlies profound humor. If all his actions and striving come to naught, if all human enterprise leads to folly, at least man is the author of his own reality. It is this sense of authority for the making of one's reality and the simultaneous recognition of limitation, weakness, and folly in one's own behavior that distinguishes humor, as a mode of consciousness, from the merely external comical. When the comical is outside the individual, as when the teller of the joke achieves laughter at the expense of the others, it is not a mode of self-apprehension. But when the comical serves as a penetration of reality which refers back to the comic figure, then its inwardness represents self-reflection and sympathy. Is not irony then a form of the comical? Yes, irony represents a highly individual-oriented mood of the comical when it looks forward to a victory over the transitory and the contingent. But irony also sees the way out in painful vision, despair over what one is and over what one would like to be. Where the unreflective man has the comical outside himself in the form of a joke external to himself and at the expense of others and the world, irony takes the comical into itself as its own condition. It detaches itself from the contingencies of the world and the latter's realm of objective knowledge, it keeps its joke secret to itself, and this enables it to hover above the world and its finitude. But because there is yet a promise for the ironic self, a future, there is suffering change and the frustration presented through its projected imagination of the infinite ideal. In irony the individual chooses the life of a despairer, chooses to become the possibility that is uncovered in the not-yet, the invisible to which he relates himself, his future, his own inner time.

The humorist opens the moment and creates the event that raises the question of human completeness, perfection. The union of the earnest and the wistful functions as a model for the union of the finite and the infinite, a model of resolution and harmony through contradiction and paradox. An element of the paradoxical is always present in the life of the humorist. It is precisely this connection between paradox and humor which has led some thinkers to assert that the mood of the humorous does not occur before Christianity, that such statements as "a rich man's difficulty in entering the kingdom of God is like that of a camel passing through a needle's eye" contain this new mood, which is built upon a discovery of the Christian experience of the eternal, the infinite—the reference to which is always paradoxical. The paradoxical in this context is the introduction of the concept of something infinite in the midst of the finite and, reciprocally, the entertaining of the finite in the midst of the infinite or apprehension of the timeless—that which is beyond time but which symbolizes the fulfillment of the temporal process. Apparently, however, from Kierkegaard's interpretation, Socrates and the Socratic humor prefigure the Christian.

The temporal is then the key element of the humorous. "Low" and "high" humor, or following Høffding's terminology, "little" (*lille bitte*) and "great" (*store*) humor are the polarities that identify the degree to which the temporal paradoxes are emphasized. The joke, the satire, and negative forms of irony (focusing primarily upon separation, individuation) fall into the category of "little" humor. But increasingly, as the more common human temporal and paradoxical condition is emphasized, and as sympathy is released into the shared event, which reflects human creativeness and human limitation—illuminating the eternal as unlimited creativeness—the more appropriate it becomes to describe the humorous, the comic consciousness, as "great" humor.

Irony acts to particularize the individual in such a way that he discovers his "eternal validity." But his eternal validity becomes his finite freedom. Irony leads to historical self-apprehension. This was how Kierkegaard began to understand the Socratic model. Humor now brings the world of others back to the individual. Universals, timeless truths, connect man with man in that they point toward perfection (ideal forms) and completion; and, because they reflect limitation, they indicate common human denominators. Kierkegaard's "existing thinker," the paradigm to which he associated Socrates, has this capacity to exercise the paradox of perfection, whether in terms of virtue, knowledge, or leadership.

When Socrates asks whether virtue can be taught and he cannot find either students or teachers of virtue (*Meno*), when he grounds knowledge upon a paradox of its very pursuit, and when he discovers the negative effects of "good" leaders (*Gorgias*), he is exercising the humorous. These events in the *Dialogues*, the eristic dialectic, were first seen as ironical movements without result and with a repelling force upon the pupil. Kierkegaard's reevaluation of the Socratic is the discovery of a greater depth of intention between Socrates and his neighbor, an uncovering of the paradoxical temporality the awareness of which serves to point to something timeless and so to shift the entire perspective of the arguments and images of the dialogue's world. It is precisely humor that transforms the temporal dimension of the understanding and puts the participants "into motion." The motion Socrates and his comrades experience is the redirection toward the eternal, the break from the circle of being which is rooted in the memory of the race. Memory is the central focus for the Greek epistemology and mythical consciousness. In Socrates' orientation toward a recollecting of the eternal, Kierkegaard rediscovers an act of humor, an act he sees as an "analogy to faith."[20]

Socrates as *maieutiker* assists and participates in the delivery of an idea to birth. The idea is, however, secondary to the phenomenon that an individual goes through a rebirth process. It is the emphasis upon process which distinguishes, at least for Kierkegaard, the Socratic from the Platonic. If primary emphasis were placed upon the Idea, as a separable entity with independent value, then the Socratic would be dabbling in the philosophy of speculation. But because Socrates opens and shares the event, is autopathic and sympathetic in his relationship with the one who is latent with new life, and because his silent vanishing—the competency of his ignorance—beckons the other to become an associate before the Unknown, Socrates' way of life signifies the thinker in existence and symbolizes the teacher dwelling in the intersection of the paradox that puts together the finite and the infinite, the conditioned and unconditioned, body and soul.

Socrates as teacher, as helper, introduces the element of temporality, the added dimension of depth. His orientation is jestingly toward the prior existence of the soul in eternity— the eternal "before," the golden age, innocence, the primordial, the cosmic mother. But Kierkegaard perceives in the Socratic jest a deeper seriousness, which he understands as an analogy to faith. And faith for Kierkegaard is the future to which the individual is beholden, is the actuality of continuity through trust in the eternal. The consequence of the analogy of faith is that in the silence that ushers in the fullness of time it is the Divine (for Socrates) or Christ (for Kierkegaard) who holds the power to complete the individual. Between man and man there is no possibility for this completion, this perfection of being. And this is another feature of the Socratic humor, that it remains faithful to the fact that individuals cannot complete one another, even in love. The paradox of the educator is that he both gives the impression and simultaneously removes the ground for this assumption.

It is Kierkegaard's notion that Socrates orients the individual to his own inward divinity. Socrates is almost a Christian, and Kierkegaard has all he can do to maintain the distinction between the Socratic teacher (the humanistic tradition) and the Christ teacher (the Christian tradition).

But Socrates disappears in the instant of rebirth. Socrates is merely an occasion, a reminder—although one reminded. Is he gone forever? The learner has made his "leap," his act of faith which places him in the instant of eternity by means of the animating power of the paradox. What happens to the teacher while the learner leaps?

3.
Socrates Witnessing:
The Trial of Subjectivity

Socrates and his pupil vanish in that fortuitous instant, the occasion of recollection, through which they and the instant itself become like grains of sand on a desert of eternity. Their disappearance functions like the ending scene of an episode in an adventure series in which the unthinkable conclusive act (the hero falls from a cliff) is apparently committed, only to be repeated at the beginning of a sequel in which it is discovered that the terminating deed was only an allusion to what might have happened and everything is somewhat otherwise (the hero is hanging from a branch over a chasm), thus permitting the series its interminable future, and the hero another episode in the passions and trials of his life. But both the dreadful and the reenacted hopeful scenes have been played. We receive the impact of both worlds: the tragic passage of the hero from existence and the comic relief of his shining reappearance gain simultaneity in the vanishing act. Socrates, accordingly, who could have taken himself back into an immanent preexistence, who could have forgotten himself for the sake of eternity, does not in fact vanish into the impersonal timelessness behind him. And the learner, who is in midair, like the hovering ironist, comes crashing down to earth in the comic gesture of existential gravity. The pupil's running leap, flight, and fall serve him as a personal metaphor for the self-integration of character. The experienced analogy to existence is that the temporal polarities of life can be neither abandoned nor isolated. Pre- and post-existence are temporal coordinates of the unity of the moment, the before and after that receive their qualitative significance by virtue of a decision. Socrates chooses not to deny the human condition, that of a finite existing thinker. In theory he and the pupil are oriented toward a forgotten immutability which they seek to recollect by the aid of hypothesis. They do not gain entrance into eternity but allow the Unknown to orient them in life pursuits. And they serve to remind one another of the journey into unknown regions lest they lapse into a second forgetfulness: the ignorance of not knowing that one is ignorant. Whatever else the eternal might be, for the existing thinker it is the paradox of pursuing self-knowledge: the desire to know the unknowable. Or, as Kierkegaard would have it, "reason seeking its own downfall." Passionate investment in that paradoxical pursuit makes it analogous to the Christian conception of belief in an eternal Being who is in himself paradoxical, the man-God idea.

Socrates' mock vanishing is an act of humorous proportion placing him at the threshold of religious life (Christianity). Resolved about and resigned to the paradoxical relationship, Socrates becomes a humorist who even makes the question of what it means to be a human being an inconclusive inquiry. The individual takes on the character of the unknown to which he orients himself, and the paradigm for this thought process manifests itself in those topics related to eternality: truth, virtue, the Good and the beautiful. These, when scrutinized, all lead the seeker back to himself in his search. The objects of knowledge remain uncertain. The thinker has only the certainty of apprehending himself seeking under the particular influence of that which he makes the object of his inquiry. Were he even to make himself the object, self-consciousness would itself remain paradoxical. It should not be forgotten, says Kierkegaard, that the Socratic orientation,

however analogous to the Christian, is different because it is
"in immanence," i.e., conceived in terms of a prior existence,
an anterior essence.

We can understand why Kierkegaard insists upon the element of immanence in the Socratic view. Though it becomes
existentially qualified as paradoxical, thus intensifying the
temporal character of human becoming, the result of a doctrine of immanence would be the point of termination in a
theory of communication. If the utmost relationship between
man and man is the occasion of reminding one another of a
preexistent knowledge of the eternal, then any further acts of
communication become unessential. Each individual becomes an isolated unit needing no other being, neither man
nor God, to assist him in his development and self-perfection. The doctrine of immanence ultimately terminates any
communication of an ethical character. The Socratic dialogue, however, does not end with the theory of recollection.
Even the theories of afterlife are given the status of uncertainty. Socrates both posits an immanent possibility and
rules out is actualization. Memory itself becomes inconclusive just as history, from Kierkegaard's standpoint, is only an
approximation of the truth.

Socrates neither hovers nor vanishes according to act three
of our drama. Or rather, he not only hovers and vanishes, in
irony and in humor, but also remains upon the scene in yet a
third role. Immanence cannot be the final answer to the question of what it means to be an individual. There remains a
third possibility for the presence of one individual to another
which implies what it means to be an existing subject. Kierkegaard introduces the terms "testimony," and for the one who
testifies, "witness," as yet inferring another possibility for
communication, which lies most truly between direct and indirect modes. The witness to the truth does not orient the
fellow being to an "instant," the emptying of time; rather, the
witness directs himself to his fellow being in such a way that
the witness turns toward God and creates the moment that is
a fullness of time. The "testimony" is therefore both direct

and indirect in that the witness addresses his communication toward his fellow creature but directs himself to God.[1] Throughout the later period of his authorship, Kierkegaard uses the terminology of the "trial" with its witness and testimony. It is also in this period that he dwells most decisively upon the category of the individual (*hiin enkelte*). The witness and the individual are subsequently brought together in what we propose as the third Socratic posture: "the single witness," the concluding posture of an educator.

The Socratic witness is prefigured in *Works of Love,* where the greatest service that one being can render another is discussed. We are to imagine the learner in position for his leap —maieutically induced. The helper who has served to facilitate this moment stands aside so as not to interfere. When the learner produces himself through a decisive act, the helper or teacher could say: "This man, by my help, stands alone."[2] Of course, Kierkegaard refers not merely to a statement but to the articulation of a type of understanding which positions the teacher in relationship to the learner. The teacher really says to himself concerning the learner, "You could not have become independent without my assistance." This inaudible utterance is no doubt covertly active in the relationship. There is a hidden dependency underlying the act of facilitation. The teacher cannot really let go of the learner for, though he wishes him his independence, he also fears the loss of the learner's affection. Love relationships that are based upon inequality cannot be tolerably terminated. This is not the Socratic standpoint, continues Kierkegaard. Socrates would have said, "This man stands alone—by my help."

What difference is there between these two statements? Is this anything more than sophistry? Yes, proclaims Kierkegaard, for what Socrates says indicates his basic attitude, that the most one individual can do for another is to make him free: "independent, unto himself, unto his own, and simply by hiding his help he helps him to stand alone."[3] Kierkegaard playfully emphasizes the function of the dash (*tankestreg*, literally, thought line) in Socrates' sentence, "—by my help." The dash indicates the Socratic concealment, "the secret of an indescribable smile," that he manages to hide his assistance in the very act. Whether it is irony or humor that keeps Socrates' maieutic art precisely an art that does not create dependency, Kierkegaard does not say. But he offers the image of a dash, the grammatical Socrates, as underlining the learner's leap. In this way Socrates' vanishing becomes a kind of hidden affirmation of the learner's independence. Is he, who in helping another also demonstrates self-renunciation, then a Christian? No, adds Kierkegaard, once again amending the Socratic posture. However noble, magnanimous, and disinterested is Socrates' attitude, still he does not, "in the sense of concern love the one he wanted to help."[4]

Concerned love, *agape* (though we note that Kierkegaard never uses this term), is reserved for the Christian helper who truly loves the learner because he experiences the eternal as a possibility in the other. There is a form of love exhibited by Socrates, a *philos*, but it is apparently more drawn to the process of individual self-realization than to what is made manifest through the relationship. Socrates gains a certain degree of satisfaction through his enabling act; but the helper whose act is truly a work of love knows that the person who stands alone does so "by God's help." His only reward is to be once more "transformed into nothingness," which is his divine blessedness.

The Socratic posture is something more than a mere vanishing, but something less than an abiding presence. The version of Socrates in *Works of Love* leaves him with his hidden smile confirming the situation of the pupil. Socrates is smiling to himself—that is the final communication of a humorist.

The case of the third Socratic posture is opened in a set of writings which, though written at various times between 1846 and 1851, remained unpublished until after Kierkegaard's death in 1855. It may seem that we are now making Kierkegaard's personal life and literary intentions the focal point of our inquiry. This is true to the extent that Kierke-

gaard makes the intention of his literary activity itself a part
of that activity. He becomes, for reasons we will mention, his
own witness. The mood and setting of the works intended to
summarize the "authorship"—the corpus of his literary
activity from *Either/Or* to some of the edifying discourses
following *Works of Love*—give the impression of a "confes-
sions" in the genre of St. Augustine or Rousseau. But the
association is also to a trial such as the one we find in Plato's
Apology. The language of a trial is strongly indicated by the
terms "testimony, witness, accounting," etc. The category of
the individual is itself on trial. It is unclear whether Socrates,
Kierkegaard, or the "authorship" is the defendent—perhaps
all three embodied in one figure, the witness.

Two events sparked Kierkegaard to produce a set of autobiographical works concerning his "authorship" and, concurrently, to attempt an intensification of the meaning of being
an individual. The two tasks were aimed at a mutual clarifi-
cation, as we shall see.

In 1846, partially through his own instigation, Kierkegaard
drew down upon himself the satirical fire of a comic weekly,
The Corsair. Dwelling upon his physical and personal idio-
syncrasies, this much less noble and more vulgar form of
satire continued to generate the parallels with the ancient
Greek—Socrates as parodied in the *Comedies* of Aristophanes. The false impression the ensuing *Corsair* articles
and cartoons gave of Kierkegaard's name and person created
a confusion surpassing the intentional ambiguity of his own
authorship. The master of indirect communication—"deceiving into the truth"—saw that his strategy had gotten out of
hand. He was compelled to offer an explanation concerning
his actual art and intention as an "essentially religious
author." In 1848 he wrote *The Point of View for My Work as
an Author*. But, changing his mind about publishing this
"direct report" until the public should have certification of
his ultimate disinterestedness in the matter, Kierkegaard
allowed the work to first appear posthumously, which it did
in 1859, four years after his death.

The second event, a literary equivalent to the Socratic "immortality" hypothesis, came with the information that *Either/Or* had gone out of print and that there was sufficient demand to justify a second edition. Kierkegaard received intimation of a literary immortality: "the first fruit comes forward a second time." Again Kierkegaard delayed the republication. Two years later, in 1849, he accompanied the second edition with the *Three Godly Discourses (Tre Gudelige Taler).* Still he refused to declare his position publically; instead he continued to balance the "aesthetical" *Either/Or* (as he did the first time in 1843) with the "religious discourses" and sermons. In 1851 he made public a condensed version of the *Point of View,* which was called *My Activity as a Writer.* The little treatise was given as if it were a kind of inventory of styles, the first section of which he titled "The Accounting" *(Regnskabet).* With "The Accounting" Kierkegaard wistfully began to reveal something of the incomes and expenditures of his literary craft. Nevertheless, what is certified leaves us, the readers, in an even more puzzling position than we were before these "direct accounts."

We are told that the "authorship" traces a movement from the poetical (aesthetic), from philosophical speculation, to the heart of that which defines Christianity. The literary production corresponding to this movement went *from* the pseudonymous *Either/Or through* the *Postscript to* the "Discourses at Communion on Fridays," i.e., from the first through to the second edition of *Either/Or,* including the accompanying "religious communication" published under his own name.[5] The strategy of his authorship was thus one of producing a double impression of the author, as a serious religous thinker and as a poetical and philosophical wit. But why should an author seek to keep his public in a state of confusion about his ultimate intentions? There are two reasons: first, to free the reader from a possible admiration of the author as a nobly religious individual, an admiration that would have placed that author in a higher position than his reader, hence defeating his whole purpose; and second, to appeal, to snare the general public attracted as it is to aesthetic and philosophic works or to the styles of interesting, proud, and clever heads, in order to put out hooks upon which certain individual readers might snag themselves.

Even in explaining the strategy of his authorship Kierkegaard does not cease to be the subjective thinker at work. He does not attempt to find an Archimedian point outside the authorship but continues to draw the concerned reader deeper into his own situation. The movement of the authorship is, as he says, *maieutic*. Yes, we understand by now that to be a Socratic midwife means to employ irony and humor, to begin with the real situation of the reader, to engage aesthetical devices, to be poetic in expressing an invitation to explore the unknowns that are present in our daily lives rather than some far-off ideas. But there is another foundation for the *maieutic* effort, one barely hinted at in the notion of reflection. Reflection is the encompassing action of the whole authorship. If we understand what Kierkegaard means by "reflection," then we have made an inroad into the dense and ambiguous language of "the individual." Let us recall that Kierkegaard, like Hegel, identifies reflection with movement of thought.

"The authorship is the movement of reflection itself."[6] Clearly, reflection is the most inclusive term and direct and indirect discourse both belong to reflection. Direct and indirect discourse refer to how reflection is communicated. Indirect communication is accompanied by a second-order reflection that is aimed at confounding and altering the recipient's sense of what it means to participate receptively. Irony, for example, aims to reduce the recipient to a state of self-acknowledged ignorance by confronting him with a paradox —a departure from his expectations. We follow the ironical character cheerfully into the incommensurable consequences of his life and are left there with the task of finding our way back or foraging on through the difficulties to which we have been attracted. A direct communication is free of this second-order reflection, but it is nevertheless an expression embodying reflection, one that assumes our ability to deal directly with its contents as ready recipients. Either form requires an appropriation process from the recipient's side. It is simply a matter of what has priority for us: the altering of our interpretive mode of engagement, or the conjoined reflective engagement with the content of the communication. Kierkegaard establishes the essential movement as from indirect to direct communication, from complexity toward simplicity.[7]

It is not simplicity but "essence" that traditional metaphysics (Hegelianism) reached through reflection. Reflection means not only that the human intellect operates, but that it is able, by turning back upon itself, to know itself and its performances. Reflection enables thought to discover itself as thinking—being discloses its essence. In establishing an identity with itself the mind increases its content in ever broader reflective concepts until it reaches the most inclusive, which is Mind itself or Spirit. But reflection has a radically different meaning for Kierkegaard and for the intrinsic movement of his authorship.

What is communicated and how it has been communicated have in common the form of reflection. Furthermore, explains Kierkegaard, what has received expression endures as such but that which is reflected in it "is taken back out of reflection" by the thinker.[8] The authorship that traces the give and take of reflection indicates, says Kierkegaard, "my own upbringing and development." Reflection, then, rather than being a way into greater and greater concentric spheres of knowledge, rather than being the action of the mind growing toward greater self-possession and identity, is the discipline that enables the individual to break with his own patterns of thought. Reflection, rather than filling up the individual with a self-conscious content, is an emptying of the content of self; it is not a negation but a loosening of its hold upon itself. Refection does not enable the individual to enter the absolute, to reflect himself into Christianity, but, instead, "one reflects oneself out of something else and becomes, more and more simply, a Christian."[9]

The reason that the authorship traces the movement of reflection is because Kierkegaard is the "reader" rather than the author. He takes himself back in reflection in order to live through the consequences of that which is reflected in his communication. The expression and its reflective life endure, but the author has unfinished business elsewhere. The authorship is a personal history made available to any person who wills to undertake the journey traced out in its pages. In "The Accounting" Kierkegaard manages to vanish as an author but persist as a reader. He formally declares himself as the future simplicity implied by that which is unfolded in the many books. By becoming his own reader Kierkegaard places himself in the position of contemporaneity with every subsequent reader.

Just as reflection is the way that an individual takes in altering and freeing the patterns of his receptivity—the discipline that breaks with the old paradigms—so the category of the individual begins to emerge from complexity toward simplicity, from the crowd toward the single witness. The truth of being that reflection delivers is "becoming." And in the account books of his authorship Kierkegaard simplifies reflected communication by turning all the mirrors back upon the reader. Reflection, like many other terms of Kierkegaard's vocabulary, can be understood grammatically: as with the case of the reflexive verb, both subject and direct object are copresent in the action. The word "individual" (*enkelt*), in the way Kierkegaard uses it, has this reflective quality built in. *Enkelt* can mean single, simple, individual, and solitary. The richness of the word is lost to us in English as is its active sense. The individual is less an entity, a discrete unit, than an orienting to action. Reflection leading to simplicity is what the authorship is when transposed into communication. Becoming singular, simple, solitary—becoming an individual—is the task of the authorship.

The concept of the individual is not one that could be passively delivered in a lecture; "it is a specific ability, an art, an ethical task, and it is an art the practice of which might in his

time have cost the practitioner his life."[10] Indeed, such a price
was paid by Socrates, who, "with decisive dialectical force"
used the category of the individual for the first time.[11] We
take up the movement of the authorship once more, Socratically enriched, in the "Two Notes Concerning the Individual"
which are appended to the *Point of View.*

Let us keep in mind the question of communication which
has been so closely linked with the Socratic postures and with
the category of the individual. We discussed Kierkegaard's
notion of Socratic aloofness in relation to the theory of recollection and how that raised the question of orientation in the
communicative arts, vis-a-vis "immanence." The decisive
meaning of the third Socratic posture, as it gradually unfolds, is a Socrates located between the extremes of the crowd
and the isolated personality, babel and silence, and between
paganism and Christianity. As a "between" form of communication, witnessing is also the between form of existential
orientation; i.e., between the limited and the limitless, the
conditional and the unconditioned, history and eternity.

Introducing the "Two Notes" Kierkegaard—the voice of
the authorship—speaks of the politician who, "if he truly
loves what it is to be a man [*menneske*, human being] and
really loves men," will become aware that the religious is the
"transfigured rendering" of that which has entered the politician's thoughts in his happiest moments.[12] With this bold
statement, connecting the sacred and the mundane more
directly than almost anywhere else in the authorship, Kierkegaard begins to say what being an individual means. He contrasts the politician with "that practical philosopher of
antiquity." There are numerous references, throughout the
ensuing discussion of the individual, to the Socrates we find
most equivalently portrayed in Plato's *Gorgias.* Kierkegaard
does not give any particular references to the *Dialogues;* his
interpretation of the Socratic is increasingly "without authority." But the language of witnessing, testimony, and being a
single witness, which echoes throughout the "Two Notes," is
echoed back from the *Gorgias* where Socrates says of himself

that he is "one of the few Athenians, not to say the only one, engaged in true political art," and that of the men of his day he alone "practices statesmanship."[13]

We know that in the *Gorgias* Socrates disputes with the rhetorician, Gorgias, and with two of his up-and-coming students of political ambition, Polus and Callicles. The issue of communication is particularly stressed in the *Gorgias* where the false ("flattering") art of persuasion (rhetoric) is distinguished from the true political art practiced by the man of virtue, the "single witness." The issue of communication in the *Gorgias* does not dwell upon recollection but upon the qualitative and quantitative mentalities, the individual versus the crowd. Similarly, in the "Two Notes," the character of crowd mentality and the individual as emergent quality are juxtaposed.

Socrates' aim is not to win the vote of many but, rather, to produce a "solitary witness to the truth" in the other.[14] And so it is with Kierkegaard who seeks to find the individual in the crowd, regardless of how many there may be, to find each one singly and to be found singly by the witness.

The conventional politican (*rhetor*) concerns himself with the many, the crowd, a quantitative infinite. And in his thinking the politician allows the quantitative dialectic to permeate every goal. How much pleasure rather than the common good, how much power rather than justice, how much knowledge rather than wisdom is his concern. The benefactor becomes a tyrant, as Socrates could foresee, since the quantitative dialectic has no inner *telos* but requires the imposition of control in order to bring about a semblance of harmony. The quantitative resists orderliness as an unnecessary restriction against its infinite efforts; it has no self-limits. Reflection in the quantitative realm can never produce results or simplicity, for quantitative reflection only serves to stir up greater desires for further possessions and satisfactions. Real needs remain undiscovered; reflection magnifies complexity. Socrates' arguments, images, and analogies in discussion with the proud Callicles are of no avail. The single witness is not produced. Callicles will not witness himself but rather claims to testify on behalf of the many, to give the popular view. The qualitative dialectic goes unborn, except in Socrates. Dialogue hints of tribunal: the quantitative view will ask for the life of the single witness. The comic pathos of the single witness is constantly in the background. Having been tried by the ungovernable mind, he is assigned the extreme punishment. But the single witness, comically, makes his own death a topic of investigation. The *Gorgias* ends with Socrates relating the myth of afterlife and its judgments, the highest tribunal—of single men before single gods in naked judgment.

The image of judgment, Socrates before his Rhadamanthus, which terminates the *Gorgias*, leaves Socrates with the questions of justice and the leading of life according to "right" precepts. But the single witness Kierkegaard seeks to be and to produce is something quite different from this Socrates.

> As a single individual he is alone, alone in the whole world, alone before God—and with that there is no question about obedience![15]

Kierkegaard's single one stands "alone before God." His mission is not fulfilled strictly by finding the "right" life, but by living *before* and *for* God in obedience to his commandments —to love God and to love one's neighbor. Socrates and Kierkegaard each take their own ways at the end of the story. Clearly, in the same moment, Kierkegaard makes a distinction between the single individual and the cults that gather around such terms as "individualism," and "subjectivism." The single one is not complete nor is he self-completing. He does not live on his own terms but in "obedience." He belongs not only to himself as a subjective thinker, but he belongs to what is higher, to God, whom Kierkegaard also calls the "individual."[16] And what of Socrates, who could not have been a Christian? Proclaims Kierkegaard, "I am thoroughly convinced that he has become one."[17] If he can say that Soc-

rates has become a Christian, then it must be because Kierkegaard refers to the Socratic in himself which he has Christian-
ized. The statement that Socrates becomes a Christian should
have forewarned us that a Socratic thinker has become the
vehicle for a Christian spirit. Actually, we should not be surprised to realize that the Socratic and Socrates function as
another example, indeed, as the paradigm, of Kierkegaard's
double reflectiveness. Socrates both does and does not love
the pupil, both is and is not a Christian, both is and is not
Kierkegaard. Either interpretation is made possible, the one
reflected into the other. The existential version of the Danish
Socrates is two-faced, bi-frontal, Janus-like: one face directed
at the romantic spirit and its ecstatic individualism, the other
turned toward the world-historical subject of philosphical
idealism. The Socratic is itself the second reflection in the
double communication of indirect discourse as well as the
clue to its decipherment.

The authorship may be Socratic, but Kierkegaard is not
Socrates. With his statement, "stands alone before God,"
Kierkegaard should have removed any remaining confusion.
He gives further indication of this in a second version repro-
ducing the movement of the authorship and its limitations in
the second note of the "Two Notes Pertaining to My Work as
an Author."

Here Kierkegaard's tactic is to disclaim that he was "a witness for the truth."[18] His approach is like that of Socrates in
the *Meno*, who seeks but cannot find teachers of virtue while
he is ironically the very creature sought after. There are three
grounds upon which Kierkegaard claims to falter in being the
witness: first, he was a member of the privileged class, not
having been compelled to work for his living; second, he was
far too much the poet to be called a witness in the strict sense;
and third, even while he was too much of a poet, he was also
too much the ethicist, too existential, to have really been a
poet. The author, or rather the authorship, lies between these
extremes. He is on the borderline between them. And this
borderline corresponds categorically to the future, to the

coming historical age.[19] Neither author nor authorship then should be mistaken for the truth. Each is striving to become that category, that view of life, which is the communication of the single witness.

The single witness is not the crowd, nor the quantitative evaluation of oneself. The single witness is a way toward God, a life of self-renunciation and devotion. The category of the individual also expresses Kierkegaard's limit: the requirement that the public, the political, the mundane beloved (friends, spouse), and generally the world are to be renounced. The last communicative possibility, the highest for Kierkegaard, is with God and with oneself. At the last, it is still unclear whether the authorship is essentially Socratic or Christian, since in his conception of love for the other, the neighbor, the reader remains secondary to, rather than integrated with, communion with oneself and with God.

PART II

Either/Or: Allegory of the Educator

> He who says "the book is entitled
> *Either/Or,"* really says nothing at all;
> but he who says "the work *is* an
> *Either/Or,"* produces the title him-
> self.
>
> —VICTOR EREMITA, Postscript to
> *Either/Or*

Preface
The Paper Duel of Victor Eremita

In 1843 a certain two-volume work entitled *Either/Or* came before the reading public in Copenhagen, a book that aroused much interest partly because of the great diversity in style and temperament of its six parts—including some very provocative writing about seduction—and partly because the book had no author but only the name of an editor, that clearly pseudonymous figure "Victor Eremita." Victor disclaimed any imputation that he might have been the author of the two volumes. Instead, he offered the following explanation. There was a certain old bureau standing in the window of an antique dealer, which, as he passed each day, he grew increasingly fond of. Finally, in a moment of acquisitive passion, he bought it. He gave it a prominent place in one of his rooms and all was well and good. But early one morning, as he was about to take a journey to the countryside, a drawer in the bureau containing his travel money refused to open. In a fit of passion equal to that when it was acquired, Victor struck the bureau with a hatchet. The drawer failed to budge, but instead a secret door sprang open. Inside was a parcel of papers. Examining them quickly he realized that here was something more valuable than money, here was access to the intimate lives of two very different sorts of individuals. He would therefore take the papers with him on his journey. But where to put them? A mahogany case was fetched which contained a pair of pistols, very likely dueling pistols. They were removed and the papers were placed inside. Victor then set off on his journey. Once having arrived at the country inn, he proceeded to a secluded place in the forest where he withdrew the papers from the dueling case and began to read them. With this the duel of the two sets of papers began. Subsequently, since he so gratuitously decided to share these papers with us, we too enter into this paper duel.

The editor, then, of *Either/Or*, Victor Eremita, claims to have discovered the papers of two unknown authors of opposite and irresolvable dispositions. He proposes to put them before us in a manner consistent with his own dialectical marksmanship.

> One sometimes chances upon novels in which certain characters represent opposing views of life. It usually ends by one of them convincing the other. Instead of these views being allowed to speak for themselves, the reader is enriched by being told the historical results, that one had convinced the other. I regard it as fortunate that these papers contain no such information.[1]

It is for the reader then to decide what the historical results of *Either/Or* might be; he must himself produce the significance of the title.

We of course have the historical advantage, or perhaps disadvantage, of knowing without question that the real author is Kierkegaard and that this is his first literary work composed in part while he was finishing that ironical dissertation on Socrates, *Concept of Irony*. *Either/Or* possesses qualities of the Socratic in that a situation of reflective contrast is opened between pseudonymous characters while any actual author remains absent. The work itself as "edited" rather than "authorized" remains unresolved, having no final results apart from what the reader chooses to imagine. The work of *Either/Or* is to evoke subjectivity by beckoning the reader to invest his sense of the possible in life, such as one might expect of a novel. It does not compel the reader to witness the utterances of a narrator and, hence, its dialectic remains something less developed than the advanced Socratic posture reached by Kierkegaard, the "witness," in his later nonpseudonymous writings. Kierkegaard considered it an "aesthetic" work since for the reader so much emphasis was placed upon possibility while the author disappeared into the recesses from which the work issued.

Either/Or poses the possibility of choice to the reader by trying to gain his interest in one or another of the characters, inviting the reader to identify with a life view only for him to discover the dialectical tension of that view when contrasted to an opposing position. The work then is educative, just as the word *educate* (Latin, *e-ducare*) means to bring out or draw out. The work of *Either/Or* is to draw the reader out into his own possibilities and to heighten his experience of standing out (ex-istence) in the light of his own uniqueness. The work, therefore, belongs intimately to our study of the educative thinker since it goes beyond a theoretical posture, becoming the literary and philosophic embodiment of one of these postures. But there is also a second, equally important reason for placing *Either/Or* in a central position in our thematic interpretation of Kierkegaard as educative thinker. The drama of *Either/Or* is constructed through the meeting of two characters and then a peripheral third one (as we shall see). One of these characters takes up the posture of seeking to enable the other to reach a qualitative alteration of his life disposition. He becomes an educator in much less than a Socratic sense even though he is primarily concerned with the ethical in life. In typifying the person who seeks to facilitate the development of another, the character of an ethical educator is itself portrayed and revealed. We have, therefore, something to learn from *Either/Or* first, as we let ourselves be caught up in the dialectic of opposing life views, and second, as we come to understand the efforts and motives of an educator who brings unique insight to the tradition of philosophical ethics while revealing something of the complex and even contradictory position of the one who seeks to help another.

Our understanding of the relationship between modes of educating and a philosophy of human development expressed as a series of life attitudes is furthered in the interpretation of *Either/Or*. Here we discover that a life attitude is not only a relation to one's world but also an interpretive stance in relation to one's self. This is exemplified through the two primary characters of *Either/Or* in their essays, letters, and aphorisms. A is the young man who seeks to dwell in the immediacies of mood and feeling, while (the elder) B, a lower-court assessor also known as William, seeks to fulfill the ethical imperatives of what he calls the universally human. The two characters are faced together, as mirrors can be positioned, to produce an infinite series of reflections. It is a certain style of self-consciousness that creates for each character these mirrorlike surfaces. The life attitudes expressed in their styles of discourse form the perspectives of world views. When they make themselves, reflectively, the object of their own views, one might expect an open and limitless horizon of meaning to arise from the identity of subject and object. In the instances of A and B, something other than a limitless capacity for self-consciousness occurs. The control that they exercise over a view of life, presented as self-consciousness, always encounters disturbing elements. These elements are precisely those that have become associated with existentialism: despair, choice, anxiety, guilt, to name a few. They are factors of human finitude which feature whenever a finite human being faces into the cosmos of infinite possibility— even if it is the infinity of the self. Self-consciousness, for these characters, reaches a limit. Kierkegaard leaves his characters there at that threshold. Life is filled with incongruities, paradoxes, contradictions—a dialectic is born. The characters of *Either/Or* have so well circumscribed themselves that they are transformed into types. B clearly shows that this typology itself can become an object of consciousness. He attempts to show A just where the "aesthetical type" fits into the structure of types of mental attitudes. When B compares these mental attitudes to a sequence of historical personalities who exemplify their age, he establishes a parallel between the advance of historical consciousness and the development of the self.

Kierkegaard is playing up that aspect of the romantic imagination which parallels historical consciousness to the process of individuation. The idea that each individual's life is a unique participation in a universal and evolving pattern of development permeates the spirit of the romantic age. Kierkegaard uses this assumption to present the idea that while stages of life are indicative of a maturation process, their simultaneous intersection in life situations more accurately describes the dialectical tension that keeps us struggling with choices we must make over and over again. Like the sides of a die, all the stages are present. With each throw a different side gives the orientation. B himself provides us with the interpretive clue when he says that "it is not the particular stage but the movement between stages that is important."[2] The underlying theme of *Either/Or* is that man has become historical to himself, apprehending himself as a life history, and that his mode of self-apprehension is the origin for philosophical attitudes that are styles of interpretation carried out even though a different and constructed philosophy may be presented by the individual to his world.

Kierkegaard's conception of the stages of life development —the aesthetic, ironical, ethical, humoristic, and the religious—are prefigured in B's delineations. But B does not himself move beyond the ethical. He does have premonitions of a "beyond" that he is unable to enter. What is notable here, and crucial to our purposes, is that the apprehension of oneself as in a stage of life along the scale of other stages becomes itself a frame of consciousness. When character and consciousness become equivalent terms, the efforts of an educator to participate in the development of another's character reveal limits in the educator's own consciousness. The interrelationship between motives to educate and passage through life stages becomes the subject of our thematic interpretation.

4.
A Revealing Education

Judge William or B, the ethical man of *Either/Or* (Vol. II), writes two lengthy letters to his acquaintance, A, the aesthetical man. The second letter, "Equilibrium Between the Aesthetical and the Ethical in the Composition of Personality," offers to A, for purposes of altering his life disposition and for his edification, a descriptive account of the formative development of individuality. The ultimate, though not always acknowledged, concern of every person is the uncovering of his own greater and universal powers to become the harmonious and balanced personality essential to a free being. The "genuine life of freedom"[1] is the work of developing one's self. This development of the self, into which B encourages A to leap, advances along a sequence of stages, which not only indicate a series of consecutive life views, but disclose the movement, animation, and transition that are necessary for a transformation of individual life experience. It is to this "inward work" that B calls A by invoking the imperative "give birth to yourself."[2] Thus the Socratic maxim "know thyself" is transformed into "choose your self." This birth of self from self, this metamorphosis, signifies the coming-into-being of an ethical personality—the requirement for the presence of autonomous being. The apparent paradox of self-creation, the very possibility of new life and the implication of the sacrifice of a former self, is the task to which the ethical man calls the aesthetical man in his ascent to becoming the fulfillment of the "universal-human."

B's description of the second birth, which is a prerequisite for the life attitude of the ethical man, exercises the kind of language which, in scriptural context, arises as the requirement for experiencing the kingdom of God. God's kingdom and man's universe make similar demands on the individual's effort to reach self-perfection. How is such an act possible? B makes use of a way of speaking which echoes the kind of dialogue which occurs between Christ and Nicodemus (John 3:3). "Must a man enter his mother's womb a second time to be reborn?" asks Nicodemus. "You have confused two realms, that of the physical and that of the spiritual," replies Christ. "It is spirit that gives birth to spirit." Nicodemus does not seem to fathom this new way of speaking for, though he continues to question each reply, he is unaware of the transformation of dimensions given in the answers. Eventually, the metaphors of the sexual and the spiritual intersect in the image of faith. Moses lifting up the serpent in the wilderness is the symbol for man's authority, which must be revealed if the eternal is to be revealed to man (John 3:14). Faith enables man to reveal the basis for his authority. The sexual and spiritually creative powers are brought to a confrontation in the paradox of new life—which self-creation betokens.

The meeting of the aesthetic and ethical in B's second letter appears to draw upon such an unmentioned source as the scriptural context cited. It makes use of the metaphorical language of rebirth and revelation to bring A into the situation of ethicality. Character (*ethos*) requires a faithfulness to one's own process of becoming. B's letter is the authorship that invites A to a revealing education.

Speaking on behalf of "ethics," B asserts that it is the "significance of life and reality that every man become revealed."[3] "Revealing oneself" as a human undertaking belongs to the same context as "choosing oneself," and these are prerequisite to the Socratic emphasis on self-knowledge.

The central issue of ethics for B is not the capacity of the intellect to know itself nor its contemplation of eternal truths. The act of decision and the capacity to will are given priority over understanding. B clearly belongs to the Kantian revolution in ethics with its shift from the primacy of the object or goal of moral action—as, for example, in Aristotle's notion of the *telos*—to focusing on the role of the subject, the moral agent whose intention to act gains philosophical priority. Acting, for B, is choosing yourself. One becomes ethical by deciding to actualize one's possibilities in such a way that the individual defines himself. By giving definition to one's life, the person reveals himself; through his action as this particular and unique self, he constitutes a life history. Life and reality do indeed become significant insofar as the individual becomes revealed because his action determines them. The individual who chooses himself also responds to a universal imperative to do so. When moral agent and moral law are conjoined we have duty.

There is some indication, as we shall see (chapter 6) that B departs from the Kantian formulation of ethics. For Kant the moral dilemma involved a person's being able to restrain the tendency of human nature to be dominated by desire and impulse. By cultivating the reflective, rational side of human capacity, these animal forces would be suppressed. But B speaks in terms of a balance (*ligevaegt*) or equilibrium in the composition of personality. An individual's duty is not to annihilate a side of human experience but to conjoin the forces of immediate feelings, the aesthetic, and reflected duty, the ethical. B puts emphasis on the development of personality through acts of self-transformation. And his language surprises the traditional ethicist by its inclusion of a full range of human experiences and conflicts, from sexual passion (lust) to anxiety to theological notions of eternal dignity. The boundaries of traditional ethical discourse are stretched to include the concrete existence of individuals expressed here by the confrontation between the aesthetic and the ethical. We soon come to realize that these are not only philosophical categories but ways of life and modes for valuing experience. The aesthetical and ethical actually come to stand for kinds of people, and Judge William, by his own account, experiences himself and A as these people respectively. B's letter aims to reveal the educative forces that might be able to unite them.

The union to which his letter points is the friendship that arises as a consequence of shared lifeviews. But to arrive at the point of sharing, a prior unity is required: the inner unity of conflicting aspects of an individual's experience, namely, A's. To enable this meeting B has taken it as his task to reveal the development of the self, by which it gives birth to itself, to A—his Nicodemus. He takes him through intricate psychological motives which shape the various life orientations. These orientations stand related within a hierarchy of needs and values, some of which are shared by A and B. Generally, the stages are divisible into two larger groups or realms, the aesthetical and ethical. Where they meet and how the journey is to be undertaken is the story B relates to A.

Judge William offers a kind of working definition to distinguish aesthetical and ethical orientations. "The aesthetical in a man is that by which he is immediately what he is; the ethical is that whereby he becomes what he becomes."[4] The aesthetical must be a function that perpetuates a sense of givenness, affirms what already is characteristic for an individual's state of being. The ethical appears to function in relation to an incomplete state of being—what one becomes, indication that one is not yet something. The aesthetical is already an end or result if emphasis is placed upon the phrase "by which"—implying passivity, something that has acted upon a man. "Whereby" on the other hand points to a means, an action, though the end is not determined in advance.

What a man is—his condition, and how he becomes something else (something more)—further distinguishes the essence of a being—his innate capabilities—from the actual result that is the sum of that person's actions. Accordingly, the aesthetic man has already been born, while the ethical

man is bearing the weight of new life. The definition is
abstract and apparently tautological. Nevertheless a difference is posited; or, rather в presents himself as that difference. He separates himself definitively from а, and between
them he opens a chasm bridged by a series of life assumptions
leading to a reunion with himself, в. To achieve that he first
strives to locate а's position.

The aesthetical man's world is not subjective; rather, it
rests in the undifferentiated sense of omnipresence gained
sensuously through a participation in the pleasurable. The
temporal, the sequential, are experienced as distractions
which disturb the preserved life of natural being. One's
nature is an infinite source of desires and gratifications. The
art that в attributes to the aesthetic is the ability to dwell in
what simply is—the conditional. Sometimes these conditions
lie within the personal realm, as with health, beauty, and
heredity. Sometimes they are perceived as external to the
center of reference, as with wealth, glory, high station, and
so forth.[5] The closer one stands related to the immediacy of
being and exploits every possibility, the richer one's life will
be. The goal of the aesthetical seems to be, from в's point of
view, the unlimited participation in the limitlessness of being,
where being is the simple gift (*gave*), the endowment of the
self—as, for example, a talent. The difficulty encountered by
this life view is, of course, anything that stands as a resistance to this egocentrism, and the limitations on the freedom
for fulfillment which all contingent factors imply. Now it is
precisely these contingent factors that pose a stumbling block
to the aesthetic man. He is dependent, to a certain extent,
upon uncontrollable factors: one grows old, health can falter,
business is poor, others are more able, pleasures become
dulled through habituation, life loses its fascination. From
the simple coherence with earthly life, a movement gradually
disperses the immediate sense of being and forces desires
closer into the center of being—a center that begins forming
as an identity of unique combinations of feelings.

The nexus of feelings and desires which distinguishes one man from another marks the change from immediacy to reflectiveness. In reflectiveness a self-identity is experienced, and motivation is directed toward a center or self and away from the objects external to it. This stage, though still not A's particular condition, functions, for B, according to the Epicurean maxim, "Enjoy yourself." Previously it was life that was to be enjoyed; that proved difficult. Now one's self is the primary pursuit, so happiness becomes a chief concern. But, is there not a contradiction here? After all, to enjoy one's self one must therefore also enjoy one's sorrows, anxieties, and losses, for certainly these are feelings that belong quite naturally to one's being.[6] How can we gain happiness from that which makes us unhappy?

The Epicurean maxim leads through its consequences over to an opposite result—the infinite aspect of experience is intensified in the contradiction of means and ends. The conditions for happiness still remain outside the individual's control. A second, amended maxim is introduced supposedly representing the attitude of Cynicism: "Enjoy yourself while constantly casting away the conditions." Eliminating the conditional features that jeopardize self-enjoyment signifies a movement of abstraction of self from the gifts and attributes of the natural (given) being. The alteration is from heaviness to lightness: instead of increasing the content of enjoyment, one lets go of what has become a burden. The cynic hollows himself out. Nevertheless, becoming lighter by degrees, his reflective enjoyment requires the conditions to cast away; he remains tied to a quantitative and finite undertaking.[7]

These historical illustrations aim to focus more closely upon the fundamental problem of the aesthetic attitude. B uses them to build up a movement consisting of a sequence of alternating maxims (the dialectical) and the unfolding of inherently contained stages of development (the immanent) through which an individual gains passage. The oscillation is between the heavy and the light, including and excluding contents of self. The movement is apparently unidirectional since the discoveries of one life view preclude a return to the conditions of a previous orientation. B aims a historical arrow at A, one intended to pierce him in the present age of his own life history.

This dialectical development advances to a forceful presentiment: Could the very center of self be transformed: It is to the total transformation of the sense of reference that the aesthetic attitude is drawn, a metamorphosis in which one gathers oneself up into an independent unity unfettered by conditions of finitude. But where could the power to enact this total change come from? There appears to be no precedent for such an undertaking and yet no other solution seems possible or adequate. And here the individual stands, concludes B with reference to his own historical age, at a zero point with no way forward and no way back. It is as if one "comes to the world both too late and too early"; the result is the feeling of nullity, a falling away from the center of one's world, a rapid aging—it is the age of melancholy, the state of heavy-mindedness (*tungsindighed*). The apprehension of loss of centeredness gives rise to feelings of recklessness (*letsindighed*, literally, "light-mindedness"); this is counteracted by preoccupation with the past, the weightiness of memory, melancholy. It is the losing of self, the negative determination or hopeless state that first reveals the underlying emotion: despair. Despair has surfaced into the historical moment for both the age and the person. With the moment of despair B pins A against his time.

The primary importance of his account, claims B, was not the particular stages, but the impelling movement that was "imperatively necessary."[8] Likewise, despair is an emotional tension as well as a structural stage. Despair first posits hope, even though it is in its negative form, hopelessness. Hope introduces the idea of something beyond the realm of self, but not external to it. Is this a contradiction—beyond but not external to self? Spatially yes, but temporally the new is beyond but not external to the present and past. *How* the aes-

thetical man will enact the metamorphosis by which all contingent conditions are internalized and transformed through
the center of being marks itself as a development toward
what B calls the ethical state. B calls A to this beyond-present-
being with the words "Give birth to yourself." Only through
this birth can A reach the freedom he seeks, the liberation
from finitude. What B proposes then is not simply a change of
stage but an experience of the advance, the movement that
introduces an imperative, "Choose yourself."

"Choose yourself!" is the repeated refrain through hun-
dreds of pages of B's letter to A. It becomes something of an
incantation, and is invoked each time a critical situation
occurs—a critical situation being one in which an inadequate
or inauthentic solution presents itself to the vulnerable self in
transition. It is crucial to an understanding of B's intention to
notice that "choose yourself" and "give birth to yourself" are
integrally connected to a discovery of a basic energy that is
available in every person. It is to the attainment of this "unifying power of personality" that B carries his discourse. It is
not so much a matter of choosing the right, "as of the energy,
the earnestness, the pathos with which one chooses." This
energy is then the "way" as well as the goal to becoming the
fulfillment signified by the term universal-human.[9]

In order to discover this source of energy, A must uncover
his situation, which, according to B, is the fragmentary character of the self which could be represented here by the frac-
tion nullity/despair . The impulse of this human situation is
toward concealment of self from the very hope it posits, in
order to cause the tension to ease; the impulse is to dissolve
this divided emptiness. There are forms for doing this—in A's
case, literary forms: irony, satire, witticism, tragedy. But
they never yield a perfect integer, namely, the individual lib-
erated from the finite, rather, the result always remains frac-
tional. B puts A in a condition of deliberation, before choice,
saying that only through acknowledging himself as lost and
empty can he become found and fulfilled.

By disclosing himself the individual gets himself revealed—

an educational situation. Nicodemus failed to ask the right questions to bring about this development. He did, however, show his conditioning. The responses were designed to reveal to him the questions he needed to ask. But, says Nicodemus, can I reach this perfection of birth by going back inside my mother's womb? Is it the eternity before separation (prenatal) that you, teacher from God, are telling me about? The problem of the moment for Nicodemus is a backward beginning, a form of recollection such as the Greeks practiced in order to gain the timeless state (*anamnesis*). The imperative to new life leads initially to the paradox of origins and beginnings. Where do I begin? You were born of water and spirit, the bag of waters broke and, like a fish, you came to the surface to grasp the first breath of air. You were begun, you cannot begin yourself that way again, you can only begin another's life. From flesh only flesh can come. But from spirit.... Think of Moses lifting up the serpent for all to see. This is how John tells it. What does Judge William say about this beginning? "By the individual's intercourse with himself he impregnates himself and brings himself to birth."[10]

If the individual is to give birth to himself there must be a kind of sexual act. He must become both the father and the mother united in himself. But, paradoxically, the self-embrace of narcissism holds fast to the center, the sameness of being, and is a love that yearns to bring time to a stop; it is a perishing in the waters from which the self first arose. How then does the individual, A, reproduce himself into new life? The question is posed in a state of melancholy; B implies that his articulation of it is only an echo to the primary call to new life which already has occurred.

Melancholy posits hope in its hopeless wish to be eternal. In previous stages of the aesthetic, a change depended upon the conditional, the "whereby" or necessary factor of the past. Melancholy, animated by despair, has its condition ahead of it as a hope, which is not yet positive (therefore, apparently impossible) but nevertheless a posited future state of being. The kind of possibility facing A is transformative;

one loses oneself to its power and becomes another self rather than incorporating it as just one more possibility over which to muse. Simultaneously, the force that looms ahead is seemingly a projection from the despairing self. B only reaffirms the requirement of the ethical: You ought to become what you are not yet—choose yourself.

The ethical grounds itself in the presentiment of newness— a metamorphosis. B's notion of the ethical realm, announced through the imperative of choice, claims its beginning in the underlying current of the aesthetic unrestfulness that he has shown to be despair. Sensuous desire outleaps its bounds by presenting itself with an unknown life form. It despairs at the possibility; there is no way back. There is neither the highest good nor the moral will at the origin of this ethic; there is foreboding and unwillingness, anxiety and emptiness.

If B has his reader, A, intrigued by this tale, he will only be slightly more astonished by the simple maxim offered to a man about to undertake the ethical plunge: "He who despairs finds the eternal man."[11] And despair, confides B, is the first real choice of the personality. Perhaps Judge William is taking advantage of his native language to give these utterances credibility. Despair, for the melancholy Dane, is the word doubt (*tvivl*) plus the emphatic prefix (*for*), hence *fortvivle*. How could A even doubt the truths of these ethical sayings? He must be deeper than in doubt, in deliberation. To choose (*at valge*) is to elect oneself as an authority, a legislator. Then there can be doubt!

To give birth to oneself means now to make oneself the authority for one's own childhood. Is the first real choice of the personality to choose one's past? The solution is too simplified, or at least premature. How does B consider the voice of the listener at the other end of his words (letter)? Does he really know the character whose ethical transformation he claims to assist?

In despair the individual has forsaken the conditions of immediate being, conditions that tie him to the finite while they secure him in identity. A has sounded the deep emptiness of his consciousness, has confronted his nothingness out of the realization that his "somethingness"—the characteristics of personality—leads only to illusion. This knowledge frees him through the power of insight to abstract himself from conditions in general. He fastens his attention on the between states of being, upon the passing spectacle, the inter-esting (*inter-esse*). There his capacity to abstract becomes a skill for the exploitation of individuals and situations. This capacity for abstraction gives him pride, albeit pride in his no-thing-ness. He is sustained by the glory gained through victory over the illusions held by others. His style is irony. The ironic attitude serves him interpretively to release "enormous energy" for his gratifications, but he indulges in pleasure only to discover in the very instant that his devotion is an act of vanity. He becomes indolent, though he holds himself free of the pain of disappointment. His irony is, from B's point of view, unfruitful, negative.

"You are constantly beyond yourself," says B. In despair A is beyond himself in his immediacy, but before himself in his eternality. He is ahead of himself in thought, but like the wind he knows neither from whence he came nor whither he is going. The indefinite instant of A's negative irony cannot control the energy it releases because it is essentially purpose-less. A is a mixture of pride and emptiness. "Put your pride in your emptiness," is B's invocation. "Your emptiness can be transformed into a fertile readiness. Choose despair."

Despairing, the individual has turned away from the en-ergy derived from the given qualities of his immediate nature. His stance is negative, toward the inner conditions of his being, and toward the outer conditions of his environment. It is with despair that one first distinguishes the "inner" and "outer"—the twin emptinesses of being. A fine temporal line separates them which the individual first recognizes as the bare outline of an autonomous being: he has only his instants and flashes of the infinite, but these light up a profile.

The task despair announces is the fecundity of the inner space that is the consciousness of one's nullity. In this instant complex motives of the psyche intersect. Some hold the view that in this moment the need for a higher form of protectiveness arises, and that protection is the shell of the ego identity. Others have the notion that the defense against the demands of lower forces, biological impulses, the uncontrollable energy of the sensuous being (libido), is achieved through a sublimation of thwarted energies. B does not call A to these tasks. He calls upon A to voluntarily give himself to the forces that condition him, voluntarily give himself to his negative being; to be his beyondness by choosing to persevere in the moment of his hopelessness. In this way he calls A to reveal rather than protect himself. And to whom is A to reveal himself? He is to reveal himself to himself as the concrete personality devoid of every freedom except the freedom to acknowledge the imperfection of his being. In the moment of such revealing the individual experiences himself as a sacrifice and he fears.

> It is as though you were caught and ensnared and could nevermore, either in time or eternity, make your escape, it is as though you lost your own self, as though you ceased to be, it is as though the next instant you would regret it and yet it could not be undone. It is a serious and significant moment when . . . one becomes aware of oneself as the person one is. And yet one can leave it alone.[12]

Can one refuse to give birth to oneself? Yes, for inasmuch as this act arises out of freedom, one is free to refuse to pass through to the life of new being. Where does one begin? How does one make the first step? The question of beginning is raised once more. Two other voices may call out to you, says B: the voice of the poet-existence and the voice of the philosopher's doubt. Each of these speaks to the problem of origins and beginnings.

B concedes that there have been some poets who found themselves before beginning to write poetry or found themselves in their poetizing. Not these, but the poetic "ideal" is the temptation to the one in despair. Participation in the realm of poetic images for one who has not and will not choose himself can only mean a sublimation of checked desire, resisted energy. Without a true transformation, the imagination is made to take on the burden of the whole man. It cannot sustain this weight, this task of having to represent the totality of one's being. The spirit rises toward its ideal existence and, to this extent, is higher than finite particularities and multiple desires. But the images of the ideal are fleeting and are challenged on every side by the confusions and finite demands of daily life. The poet-existence is then a hovering midway between the finite and the infinite. It is an unhappy life whose sole joy is to behold the images of the ideal as they are reflected on the surface of the transitory world. The poet-existence, understood in this way, demands a protectiveness. It cannot find a way to reach the fulfillment of the ideal and so hides itself in the imagination rather than revealing itself as inadequate. The path of the poet-existence cannot represent a true beginning because it remains fearful of the deeper sources of life energy. The imagination functions to leap from the desirable to the ideal, but it sacrifices reality rather than transforming it. In the movement of sublimation of desire into the language of the ideal, the poet-existence has desexualized rather than impregnated itself. The poet is embryonic, but there will be no birth. A must choose another beginning.

Despair (*fortvivle*) and doubt (*tvivle*) have similar etymological origins or roots and a certain resonance suggests a beginning might be made through the path of rational intellect: a doubting oneself back to the origins and sources of life energy. "Doubt is the inward movement in thought itself," declares B, with a certain Cartesian echo in his voice.[13] It bears a resemblance to despair in that it strives to suspend the assumptions and motives by which it proceeds, in this sense it too is a movement toward a consciousness of nullity. However, one assumption it does not suspend, that thought can bear the full responsibility for the whole personality and find a first principle that will serve as a resting point and source for the whole of one's being. In the poet-existence the individual was prepared to abandon the rational for the sake of the imaginable. In the realm of the philosopher's doubt the nonrational, i.e., processes that do not follow certain laws of necessity, will be forsaken so that the rule of reason can triumph.

Can the personality be grounded in doubt when the aim of doubting is, from the first moment, the seeking of first principles that will be recognized by their logical necessity and sufficiency? Where is the freedom to choose when what is presented is the logically necessary? Its first moment presupposes or anticipates its conclusion: from doubt to certainty, the absence of doubt. Despair, on the other hand, is certain of itself as a nullity, and for it to doubt, it would have to postulate some thought or idea that it might suspend. Doubt suggests that despair should see itself as a necessity and by rational means ascertain its consequences. But, replies B, "despair is a doubt of the personality," while doubt is only a despair of thought.[14] Thought does not constitute the whole personality, whereas despair is a totally penetrating mood revealing, if only negatively, the whole personality in its emptiness. Therefore doubt cannot constitute the beginning for the inclusive process that despair calls for. The process of doubting may discover an absolute, unconditioned, and fundamental beginning point for thought. It may be able to reveal a rational ordering that the mind can grasp, and, insofar as one has the requisite talent to perform this feat, it may grasp the totality conceptually understood. The doubter may reach that certainty to which his intellectual talents allow him, and, in this sense, his certainty has a relative relationship to the absolute.

Individuals distinguish themselves by the degree to which they can doubt and obtain a result. Thereby, certain thinkers will have a greater claim on the absolute than others. The philosophy of doubt leads to a hierarchy of achievements and an inequality among men. How will it then reveal the universal-human? The order that the philosophy of doubt uncovers locates each man as an isolated entity in an objective absolute. The individual belongs to a system of universals but he himself is not the universal man. He may think the absolute, but his thinking carries him away from himself to a truth that is greater than but divorced from himself. The inner emptiness is concealed by the concepts that reveal the outer objective order. The consequence of the philosopher's doubt, one can infer from B's discourse, is that the language of the inner and outer sense of self is frozen into the contradiction of a "relative absolute," and into the situation where the rational intellect must dominate the personality in order to achieve the movement toward the absolute—where the absolute was the unconditioned free being. The task that B proposed, made specific by the editor's (Victor Eremita's) title, was the "equilibrium" in the composition of personality. But the process of doubt seemed to lead to a disequilibrium within the context of the personality and between man and man. "Choose despair and you choose the absolute," is B's refrain. He calls A back to the task of giving birth to himself.

The "absolute choice" lies at the heart of B's ethical theory and imperative. But what is absolute: the object to be chosen (highest good) or the way of choosing (moral will)? If the clue to A's task is the choice of a self in despair, then the absolute must be the unconditioned act, the process of choosing. The issue is not to choose this or that, not to choose the rational intellect or the powers of imagination, but to choose *with* reason and imagination—oneself. Nor is it for A to find certain shortcomings and disappointments over which to despair; for then despair has been explained, but not resolved. The requisite act for the birth of self from self is the unconditioned act in which despair itself is chosen. How can A choose despair while precisely in that state of mind that relinquishes the power of choice altogether, i.e., despair? If the power of transformation is already present in the one who despairs, and if he is only to persevere despairingly until he is metamorphosed, then the theory of new life dwells in immanence.

A doctrine of immanence in relation to the birth of self means that the development is predetermined in the conditions and therefore follows a necessary course to that end. Such a doctrine of immanent transformation embodies a developmental logic that must be understood under a category of necessity. The absoluteness with which A is supposed to choose is thus undermined; the condition is already present and an act of choice experienced as freedom is actually predetermined. When B rejected the philosophy of doubt he invalidated the kind of procedure which would make choosing oneself a mere link in a series of gradual advances upon the ethical.

Does B really understand the difficulties involved in choosing to despair while in despair, to despair despairingly? Implied in his relationship to A is the role of helper or teacher. B ministers to what he thinks are A's needs. Will his descriptions and exhortations somehow enable A to give birth to himself? Can B empower A while A lacks precisely this power to choose? Judge William begins to reveal his own situation when he writes autobiographically of the development of an ethical self. Is this the essential act between two persons—to reveal themselves to one another, to mutually empower one another? B is almost silent on this issue; at the end of his letter he will make some particularly revealing remarks. But, first he attempts to draw A into a tangle of terminology certainly more labyrinthine than the convolutions of the birth canal.

> So, then, in choosing absolutely I choose despair, and in despair I choose the absolute, for I myself am the absolute, I posit the absolute and I myself am the absolute; but in complete identity with this I can say that I choose the absolute which chooses me, that I posit the absolute which posits me.[15]

The story that B tells A, about how he apparently gave birth to himself (chose himself absolutely), involves the two in a whole set of additional characters. Each character is a movement of self-advance which proceeds as follows: first, I choose despair while in despair; in this double despair I find that I choose the absolute—that I choose absolutely—then, second, I find that I am the absolute that I posited; third, the absolute that I posited reflectively seems to have posited (chosen) me. How many different selves is B? First, he is the immediate self in despair; second, he is the self that chooses despairingly to be this despairer; third, he is the absolved self, which incorporates the two former moments; and, fourth, most paradoxically, he is again this resolved third self but this time experienced as posited by another factor, i.e., "the absolute which posits me." This is indeed a "composition" of the personality, and it is to this delivery that B would be midwife!

B's schemata for the birth of self, understood as choice, involves the dialectic of separation and reunion. He separates himself into a sequence of moments and is reunited by the impetus of released energy which offers itself to the process. Choosing activates the energy sources of conditioned being. The state of despair (the mood) is at first passive. Choosing, willing, to let despair be despair, activates the mood—an intending act in which the will wills its lack of freedom (freedom understood here as the ability to do self-work). Only by deciding to be its own condition does the self get born anew. This means accordingly that choosing and self-consciousness are identical when the choice is absolute. To choose absolutely is to practice selfhood, to legislate from and toward a center of being. Where does the power come from that makes the effort "despair/despair-chosen" possible? If the energy is already present and liberates itself (is the power) then the doctrine of immanence is asserted. To clarify this problem of movement, B undertakes to describe the nature of self.

What then is the self? First, it is freedom, says B. Most abstractly understood, the self is that which a person does not wish to alter or give up though he would change all else in the world and all circumstances of life. This is an abstract account, because the self thus expressed is an essence defined negatively: that quality which, if subtracted, would mean the disappearance of the thing examined. More correctly understood, the self, given the foregoing description of choice, is a set of tenses: the act of choosing, the chosen, the chooser, and again that which is given to choice from beyond itself (for which English might have roughly the equivalent term, the "bechosen"). Like the language that expresses it, the self I choose does and does not exist before my choosing it. Second, I do not create myself, but I choose myself and that self was created. Third, the self I choose is the most isolated of beings; yet, in the moment of its deepest solitude, it further reveals a self-continuity and relationship with all other beings.[16] What do these paradoxes of self show? If A, like Nicodemus, were present at the reading of the letter, he might have asked: "How is this possible?"

B bids A to remember the distinction with which he initiated the journey to the ethical: the aesthetic depends upon *what* a man is in his immediacy, the ethical depends upon *how* a man becomes what he becomes. The aesthetical man tries to hold on to what he already is, the ethical man wills to release himself into the task of becoming himself. The logical distinction of the paradoxes of self are clarified for the individual who recognizes that the birth process is evolved through time.

When the despairer chooses despair he transforms a present condition into a state of presence to self; he elects despair and makes himself its authority. In this sense he ceases to abstract himself from conditions of unfreedom, instead he gives himself over to the condition. Leaving aside for the moment the difficult problem of how this is made possible, and noticing that the paradoxes accurately locate and preserve this mystery, B simply informs A that what he is relating can be stated by every man who wills to do so, and that every man is obliged to will this transformation.[17] The difficulty that people have in comprehending the birth of self from self is that they use plant life rather than the human life cycle to provide them with an appropriate symbolism. The plant becomes what it immediately is, its development is immanent and cyclical. The plant comes from a seed and it makes seeds—this is visible. But where does the human being come from and where does he go? To understand this we think of our own parents and of ourselves as parents. The task, says Judge William, is "to produce oneself as the product that one is." The key to the mystery of new life is offered in the paradoxes of self. When an individual in despair chooses despair he makes himself historical by making a determination in time by which he relates himself to himself while holding on to the difference. The paradoxes of self reveal the temporal character of being.

Despair is the encounter with unfulfillment, with impossible wishes. Where does this inability come from? From the resistance of environment and from the incommensurability of means and ends in the personal dimension. The condition in which the individual finds himself is given. The given character of a person represents conditioned energy when the conditions are not also willed. Thus, for instance, a talent that cannot also be willed serves no purpose and remains unmotivated. To choose oneself as the conditioned ability to work (energy), as incompleteness of being, is to decide to have a past. The self one chooses in despair, that both does and does not exist before I choose it, is the concretely given person who experiences himself as determined or caused by factors outside his control. The self that is thus identified was created, and having been created is an unyielding fact, i.e., necessity.

When I choose myself I decide what I *have been* by deciding what I am not-yet. The immediate experience of my needs and desires becomes an unfulfilled historical past disclosing to me my task, i.e., my future. The being that immediately is becomes the being that is not-yet fulfilled. This past self *is* in the sense that it has been created, and is the conditional structure of my immediate being. I exist before my choosing it because I am not conscious of my createdness as rooted in the past. I experience it as an indeterminate present, an instant without parents and without its own death. When I choose despair I choose my parents, society—the background that reaches to the very fact of my own creation. I reenact these as the historical conditions that designate the incompleteness and hence task of my being. My being lies in becoming—I choose to be this being that is constantly ahead of itself. Choosing despair I choose my lack of freedom. I choose to hope in a freedom that Has not-yet happened. By choosing the experience of an unfree being as myself I transform the structure of my being and the way I structure and value what I see. These value structures become transformed in a temporal dimension of experience: my history. As such they gain a connectedness. My autonomy is grounded in just this act of giving continuity to the aspects and relationship of events that comprise my life. Just at this moment, explains B, when it would seem that the individual most thoroughly isolates himself, "he is most thoroughly absorbed in the root by which he is connected to the whole."[18]

The separation signified by rebirth is the individual's removing himself from his natural immediacy, his innocence. He becomes isolated, estranged from the familiar world, and is "naked as a newborn child." In the following moment of this second birth he is reunited with the whole of his particularity and is clothed again. This time he experiences the world as his own doing. The root connecting to the whole is his participation in the universal quality of finite being through personal history. The absolute choice reveals the individual's participation in the infinite as finite freedom.

The description of the metamorphosis by which the aesthetic individual integrates himself in the form of an ethical-historical person leaves the moment that the despairing individual becomes empowered, unexplained. B shows that for there to be a beginning for this process of rebirth the individual must make a determination in time and that determination takes the form of a conclusion—he "produces himself." To conclude one's life at a definite moment and as a definite event implies that change in personality is not mere repetition of sameness but is experienced as development—breaking through to newness while retaining the knowledge of the old self. Freedom, choosing the absolute that chooses me, means being released from conditions over which one has no power. While freedom is aroused fear responds as the possibility of loss of self. Individuality is threatened with extinction. The conditions against which the individual struggled nevertheless served protectively as a defense against such "unreasonable" demands as rebirth. To forsake this protection and sense of uniqueness requires courage. Detaching oneself from mother and father, from society and culture, from the conditioning powers that seem to have given the experience of each instant its particular shape, occurs when the individual chooses to attach himself to historical consciousness, to transform his dependency into his roots of growth. What power and courage animate this movement? Judge William must have some idea of the possibility of orienting another individual to enable that individual to come into his own metamorphosis. If the power of metamorphosis is immanent then A has no real need of B, or at least the relationship is a superficial one.

Judge William does not resolve the paradoxes of self-renewal, he affirms the principle of contradiction which his ethical imperative ("Give birth to yourself") uncovers. He shows that paradox to be a creative principle when understood as an act of will rather than only a moment of thought or mediation. The discontinuity of the ethical advance, from B's point of view, is the movement beyond the limits of reflection. An individual leaps into the paradoxical situation of rebirth; he falls into the historical dimension, reborn.

"Repentance" is the expression B uses to describe the act of giving birth to the free historical being. He breaks forth lyrically in Christian doctrine, introducing the transcendent category, God, as the power that responds to absolute choice positing the self in its absoluteness. The individual is absorbed into the radical incongruity that connects him to his paradoxical nature. "He repents himself back into himself, back into the family, back into the race, until he finds himself in God."[19] Repentance points to the movement of rebirth as a return to self, a looking back upon oneself in responsibility. But the self that looks back could never be derived from the looked-upon self; it derives its power "out of the hand of the eternal God." The new self, accordingly, does not judge the life around it, but, internalizing its conditions, the self experiences guilt. Creation and Fall are simultaneous. The ultimate price the ethical man pays for the integration and liberation signified by self-renewal is the estrangement from infinite freedom and the location of his domain in finite freedom. He has lost his innocence.

The radical incongruity of the ethical choice is matched by a radical break in the continuity of B's letter. Without hesitation he questions A: "What is a man without love?"[20] The love by which God is loved signifies the relationship of repentance to new life. In order to acquire his new self, when the individual is in greatest need, his next action must be to give even more of himself. Throughout his letter, B has referred to GIVING birth to oneself rather than TAKING on new identities and powers. Is it possible that to choose means to give oneself first? Is this the reason B has insisted that a letter is the best form of communication for what he has to reveal to A, because A must not make the mistake of giving himself to B, either in disagreement or agreement, but must give himself absolutely to his own process of becoming free? To love beyond the love of that which one already is, implies B, is the way to new life. To give oneself to one's createdness, to finite existence, is to make of oneself a history. In that history the individual liberates himself from the love of what he already is and from the love of his lack of freedom.

History, as man's self-work, reveals his "eternal dignity" and is the divine element from which his life unfolds. B calls upon A to become autobiographical, to see his life as a constantly unfolding story and to appropriate all the elements of that story into his life work. What kind of life would A's thus become? He would becme an "ordinary" person, says Judge William like myself. He would surrender the ideal of heroism and, with greater courage, become a friend to mankind. He would see his talent as a calling to life's tasks—his duty toward himself and other men. He will find all women in one woman in marriage. These elements characterize the fulfillment of the universal-human. They are the forms of self-legislation which the new self recognizes.

B would like A to become his friend, to share a commonly held positive view of life. But here B's wife may prove to be the more insightful analyst than the Judge. She identifies A's essential weakness as a "certain lack of womanliness," a pride that prevents A from devoting himself to anyone and anything.[21] While B disagrees with his wife on the reasons A apparently lacks a male/female equilibrium, he does acknowledge one final difficulty: though one wills to become an ordinary man, to fulfill one's universal attachment to life, an individual may in some way be unable to come through to a full realization of the obligation to be ordinary. The remaining pages of his letter carefully consider the possibility of being an "exception" to the universal-human.

The modest life of the ethical man which Judge William offers to A seems free of the fears that were encountered in passage from the aesthetical to the ethical. B has time on his side in giving absolute value to marriage, vocation and friendship. Furthermore, he has an idea about the hierarchies of development which provides him with a model with which to chart a course through life's dialectical tensions. The difficulty of the decision and the source of help in getting under way in the case of the man who would give birth to himself remain unexplained. Perhaps no explanation is necessary, nor even possible. Does the transcendent power always respond to the immanent process? B seems secure in his faith. But does the ethical man encounter difficulties? If B can guarantee the success of the journey to the ethical does he not make the transcendent power subservient to the immanent process?

The ethical man has an "energy of consciousness" that enables him to see the universal in the particular, enables him to release the possibility of the totality from the part displayed. It could be the case, however, that a man might will to translate a particular desire or intention into a universal life-form and be unable to accomplish this effort. It is possible, B concedes, that a man may not, in some way, be able to realize an aspect of universality and may instead be wounded, suffering the sorrow of incompleteness and imperfection in striving toward becoming an ordinary fulfilled human being. Eventually, though he chooses himself and repents, rejecting the negative with the whole of his being, he may encounter the very limitations prescribed by his freedom. Such a man will experience himself as an "exception" to the universal-human. In his estrangement, says B, he will be an "extraordinary" man who knows that he has "reached the confines of his individuality."[22] In one way or other every man is an exception to the domain of the universal-human. But B is reconciled to this by the fact that for such men what was lost in inclusiveness may turn into a gain in intensity.

Thus, the introduction of the concept of the "noble exception" defies recourse to "righteous rationality" in which B has invested his trust: it results in the setting up of a new dialectic of rebirth, and it is toward this that B stands oriented at the termination of his letter. But whether or not he chooses to enter upon this new pathway remains ambiguous.

5.

The Character of an Educator

One can often see the character of the person who judges others revealed in his judgments.
—KANT, *Critique of Practical Reason*

When Judge William calls upon A to "choose yourself!" he not only invokes the imperative that should orient the aesthetical man to a birth process in which a higher self comes into being but also reveals his own vocation as the educator of A. When one man calls upon another to alter his life's disposition, he evokes a situation in which each participant strikes an educational posture, even if that posture be one of resistance. In the foregoing essay, the stages of a journey were seen to illustrate the development of an ethical person from an aesthetical condition. A's task was announced through a series of invocations contained in B's long and arduous epistle. B would convert A to the life form of an ethical man. But not, he further clarified, in order for A simply to assume a different stage of development, to fulfill a predetermined role as a socially responsible individual, but for a release of energy to take place signifying the liberation of the aesthetical man from the conditions and assumptions that have served him as a form of identity, but that have also tied him up and prevented him from breaking through to another dimension of ability and freedom.

This letter-writing magistrate implies that he knows a goodness that transcends, while integrating, the stages that center upon the pleasures of immediacy. He infers not only that a dramatic alteration of A's position is required, an act of self-creation, but that a simultaneous return to self must occur, signifying a fundamentally new interpretive ground of experience laid, marking the self-transcendent drive of an individual toward a greater degree of participation in the universals of existence: hence, the universal-human. This self-transcendent function, which he calls A to discover, only occurs by the individual's first revealing himself, the act in which a historical presence to self first genuinely arises as a formative experience. When the individual first recognizes himself as the one who makes a difference through the acts of his being, he gains an inner narrative voice, he becomes a historical consciousness.

Judge William has elected himself as A's guide. His sketches of aesthetical dispositions are mimes, one running into the other—the smile gradually turning to a frown, the frown to a smile, until the tragicomic mask of A is itself portrayed. Then, B shows his own face. By contrast, the demeanor is serious, neither smiling nor frowning, mainly calm and collected, but with a tendency—shown in the brows and raised finger—toward lyrical enthusiasm and moral indignation. What makes a face convincing? What is there about the voice of true speaking that draws one into its world, advancing ahead of one's usual hesitation which considers the truth of statement?

When an educator uncovers something truthful he creates a special moment, an occasion in which he personifies the truth. He reveals something of himself, becomes transparent so as to let what is uncovered shine through. He comes to stand beside the event to share it. In a sense he discovers himself historically, autobiographically; he symbolizes the truthfulness to which his act points. The student might find the symbol, his teacher, more interesting than the truth he points out. How did he learn to make this moment actual? Could I learn to perform such feats? asks the student. Can the teacher tell how he comes to be able to be transparent—without vanishing altogether?

The editor of *Either/Or*, Victor Eremita, does not provide the reader with additional information concerning the mutuality of this educative situation. Whether A gets reborn into the ethical, whether he even accepts B as his teacher, whether B falls back into the aesthetical attitude—these speculations, which may occur to the reader, are left unresolved. We cannot help wondering about the outcome of an intimate situation about which we only know the ingredients. His letter makes us feel B's intimate assumptions. How else could he begin at one end by accusing an acquaintance of being "merely a relation to others," having no real inner personality at all, and then proceed at the end of his letter to hope for a deepened friendship?

One begins to suspect B's motives, or at least to wonder about them. What makes a man choose himself as another man's teacher, especially in this context in which the student is perhaps more clever, more eloquent, and more familiar with the dark sides of life, as B. himself admits? B cannot himself give birth to A, but he wants to be part of that occasion. He even acknowledges the possibility that an individual may be so "inexplicably woven into relationships of life which extend far beyond himself" that the riddle rebirth poses may never be guessed.[1] Nevertheless, he pursues A into the depths of the aesthetical world, striving to win him over. B is compelled and attracted to A's condition, just as some men are especially attracted to pregnant women.

Judge William describes A as like a "woman in childbirth." Every birth is miraculous to those who are involved. B gets involved by using his theories of stages and development to encounter A's aesthetical world, seeking to embrace the entire domain of that life view. The aesthetic remains a vital dimension of B's life, as his expressiveness bears out. He has apparently unified pleasure and duty, immediacy and reflection, the finite and the infinite, in the reconciliation of the ethical. He even makes the appearance of the moral good contingent upon his existence when he proclaims, "The good is for the fact that I will it, and apart from my willing it, it has no existence."[2] He constitutes his own end, he makes himself the goal of his teleology. How does A become a concern for B's teleological interests? Are there any clues?

Two phenomena reported in B's letter seem to invite an effort of character analysis, an analysis in which the reader tries to write the rest of the story. One is the mystery of the renewal of self, which remains unexplained. The second is the dialectic evinced by the incommensurability between "repentance" (the repentant individual) and the "exception" to the universal-human.

Self-renewal, though described by B, has been made A's task. Nothing more will be learned about its dynamics unless Victor Eremita produces a further report. On the other hand, the extraordinary man—who is an exception to the inclusiveness of his own apprehension of the universal—would, if he were to report on his sense of having a unique destiny, give a deepened understanding of an ethical attitude, which proposes such duties to self as rebirth.

Judge William establishes the circularity of self-movement as: from self, through the world, to self.[3] Decisiveness breaks the circle of sameness (self-identity) making a determination in time which, though a discontinuity, advances the circle of self-becoming to a qualitatively different plane. The aesthetic individual has already abstracted himself from the world, from the particular conditions of family, race, environment, and so forth. His new movement is characterized by B as repentance: he recovers and renews his world by infinitizing it, willfully removing the negative judgments that define him in relation to it. He returns to an apparently determined context, which he now experiences as the dimension of his opportunity. He has come home to himself and, in the absoluteness of choice, foregoes the innocence of first acts.

The new man participates his freedom in these finite conditions, deepening himself until he reaches a new ground, the ground of givenness itself, namely, God. The world, prepared correctly, becomes a place for grace to be received. The metamorphosis produces the man-into-world. Through the world to oneself, without sacrifice of world, is the ethical man's situation: through world to self, a repeated act of newness, an energy of consciousness.

The movement from self to self-world, the personal appropriation of the old in newness, is the essential focus of A's leap. Judge William has both feet on the ground: he has leaped. His further concern is expressed in the movement from self-world to world-self—the universalizing of personality. Judge William saves the final difficulty of the ethical for the last: the experience of incongruity between one's limited self and the total life-world that one has oneself recognized. Estranged from his own highest fulfillment, the individual dwells in imperfection; he is an exception in a certain way to the domain of universality. Here destiny meets freedom: the energy of consciousness expands itself to a limit.

The character analysis of B must approach its subject through a study of personal limitation. The tension of the shape of his being may provide an insight into B's self-appointed work as A's educator of subjectivity. Does B make himself at all transparent to A on the question of final limits? B gives an autobiographical account of his character, developed in childhood, come through to ethical-philosophical purposiveness. Intending to educate morally, B makes A his concern in later life.

Ethical earnestness is already present in the five year old, "little" William. The energy and passion to master his first lessons has been aroused through the impression of his father's serious-mindedness. The key to ethical precocity, says the matured William, is the total sense for the meaning of duty, which comes to the child at an early age if the number of particular duties is small enough that the principle of duty itself can be experienced by him. By the time little William entered the Latin School at the age of seven he had grasped this principle. The early childhood relationship with his father had instilled an intense feeling of duty in the little one which protected him from the injurious effects that might have been sustained by contact with malcontented students at the Latin School—students who complained about their teachers and could not always get along with them. "I beheld the marvellous event of a pupil being taken out of school," relates the older William, and even at that early age he affirmed the strong sense of justice which such an event signified. The expelled pupil refused to put himself under the school's discipline; he made himself an exception to the rules and to duty. Therefore, says B, "I felt that he must be an exception unworthy of my attention."[4] The little William knew only one duty, to attend school. Not even if his father were to die would the little student have ventured to avoid school, for his "father's shade" would have seemed to follow him.

Similarly, Judge William identifies his capacity for philosophical insightfulness with the early father-son relationship, a relationship based partly upon fear and partly upon admiration for the father. The unilateral obedience and respect for his father grew out of a certain manner between father and son, such that the father would simply say, "William, when the month is up, you are the third in your class." Apart from this command, says B, he never asked, never heard, never looked, never reminded, and never came to aid the little pupil.[5] But, adds B, that he hid his deep concern so that I might be matured by responsibility, is certain.

There is already a definite content for analysis in this first portion of B's personal history—a content that almost speaks for itself. There is the devoted son dominated by his father's heavy seriousness. No female figure is reported, so that an even earlier teacher of moral goodness and duty is excepted from his story. Whether then in childhood or later in adult life William came to considerations of his father's death (apparently he is still alive) is uncertain. He inserts the thought in this context, realizing that the powerful force his father represents has already made its permanent impression upon him. Even the death of the father would not release the hold his image has on him; a ghostly father figure would continue to haunt his actions. Little William bears a certain

resemblance to Hamlet, though he has claimed elsewhere to
have disdained the role of tragic hero. B's experience of his
strict and distant father is expressed by the repetition of the
phrase "he never." The explanation, intended to justify the
father's behavior on the ground that all was intended to develop the son's feeling of responsibility, is unconvincing.
Something is fermenting beneath the surface of this ethical
man's autobiography.

The father's righteous attitude and the resultant effect on
little William helped him to organize his emotional life early,
to regulate his affective life establishing the childhood will
that could control the energy aroused by reverence. "Under
this influence I regarded my father as an incarnation of the
rule," continues B; all claims arising from other sources not in
agreement with his command, little William spurned as
exceptions.

The discipline and rigor embodied in the Latin language
gave the form of law to what had been William's childish reverence. Latin grammar taught him the corollary to what he
had learned in the father-son relationship: the strict requirement that the rule and the exception are to be clearly distinguished. This knowledge of law and exception formed, in the
seven year old, a basis for making philosophical judgments.
These judgments are turned, later in life, upon another
"exception"—another pupil who puts himself outside the
obligation of universal duties and rules, namely, A.

According to B, personality emerges simultaneously with
the apprehension of duty. Duty enables the individual to sub-
mit the impulsive self to a discipline. The self is, evidently, a
more primitive center of being than personality, one which
appropriates everything to its world rather than, as in the
case of personality, going out from itself to a world it also
belongs to. Duty draws one into a world commonly shared.
The man who pursues the feeling of duty into concrete par-
ticulars, i.e., *his* duty, will be "autodidactic as well as theo-
didactic." He will teach himself and be taught by God

through this autosubmissiveness. The son is submissive to the father. The father is the incarnation of rule. Who gives the rules? God is the authority who gives rules to mankind. Is father also God? For most children the father is a godlike figure. But the morality of obedience, or heteronomy, experienced in early childhood usually leads, at about school age, to a mutuality of respect gained in the associations with childhood comrades. The rules of a game link the players together. However, little William does not seem to have experienced this transition of mutual respect and autonomous moral will in the context of his fellows. Autonomy ("Choose yourself!") becomes the catechism of his own moral teaching, but the social context in which mutuality might be developed is left unreported. Little William only sees himself in relation to the exception—as *not* the exception, but an emulation of the rule. The rule is later expressed by the grammatical utterance "either/or," the schism that distinguishes him from A. When he announces his "either/or," B becomes the incarnation of the father—the figure in whom all authority rests. B, the mature William, seems to experience himself as a second-order incarnation. His introductory phrase to the autobiography of an ethical consciousness is, "In relation to himself a man is not his uncle but his father."[6]

The ethical man fathers himself. He models himself and gains his energy from his own father's authority, a will he would never violate.[7] The unconditioned respect of the child is nevertheless heteronomous. Its determinations of moral acts (duty) are based upon external forces; for however internalized they may have become, without a transformation at the ground of moral will, the kind of respect that is fostered takes its origins outside itself and is thus conditioned. Usually, later in childhood (i.e., adolescence) a rebellion takes place overthrowing or at least suspending the father's rule. The youth seeks to discover his own equivalent of moral will, thus constituting the formative experience of personality. There is a leap from heteronomy to autonomy. This leap is not reported in в's account. Instead, one gets the impression that a father image was gradually reproduced in kind: no resistance was offered.

в's reincarnation of his father's rule has its parallel with the idea and identification of the exception. He stresses the indignation he felt toward the malcontent, the expelled pupil, as well as toward those violations of rules of grammar. As long as he remained obedient he kept himself inside the province of the rule, the domain of his father's authority. At the end of his letter, в explains to а that every man, each in his own particular way, is an exception to the universal rules or forms of existence. He does not, however, explain what kind of an exception he himself is. And, in fact, he seems to have fulfilled all the areas of universality: marriage, vocation, and fellowship. Here, in the autobiographical sketch, a source of conflict appears. How can a man become his own father without replacing him? If he replaces him there remains no standard of quality by which to judge oneself; in addition to which, one suffers the guilt of displacing the father through incarnation. But, if the father is not replaced as primary authority, the personality cannot mature into the autonomous agent of self-rule.

The exception, like the rule that becomes law, is interiorized. It is no longer others who are exceptions but oneself who is in some way outside the realm of perfect being. One is oneself both rule and exception. The authority that the son inherits from the father is a finite one, the task is infinite. In the child's eyes the father's authority is boundless and omnipotent. But for the child who becomes a father (who gives birth to himself), the scope of authority is limited. This is the knowledge of fathers and the ultimate source of their humility. When the son replaces the father as the figure of authority he loses the innocence symbolized by the childhood image of father's infinite rule. A double guilt is experienced: one stemming from the loss of innocence that the knowledge of the possibility of doing wrong brings; and one stemming from the act in which the son puts himself outside the domain of the father's authority by becoming an equal and mutual lawmaker/law-follower—the act of making oneself an exception to the father, a justification that enables the individual to transcend the finite guilt contained in the son's need to legislate for himself. Without a transcendental principle this development appears foreordained as simply an immanent process, the determining forces of which are explained by various systems. The very basis for the newness of authority requires a transcendental principle. The ethicist posits a Supreme Being: God, the infinite father. Ethics, and ethical actions, require a faith in a Supreme Being in order to gain a perspective on the authority of mortals. Could there arise a disparity between these two realms of authority, the ethical and the religious?

Judge William implies this conflict in his doctrine of repentance; there the personification of his concept of a Supreme Being is revealed. One and only one sorrow could cause B to suffer despair: the discovery that repentance was a delusion —not a delusion concerning one's own guilt and desire for forgiveness, "but with respect to the accountability forgiveness implies."[8] The primary difficulty for the ethical man lies not so much in his relationship to the conditions of mankind —the loss of innocence, participation in the history of the race—but in his belief in a being to whom one is accountable, i.e., the Supreme Being, God the father. If one is not accountable then there was no purpose to becoming one's own father, an unforgivable act between father and son. The story is the obverse of the Abraham one: the son hears a command to sacrifice the father (his authority) even though he is eternally indebted to him. Perhaps, as in the Abraham story, another command will stay the hand of the son who has proven his faithfulness to a higher authority.

The foregoing are only conjectures. B tells something, but not quite enough, for a character analysis to find sufficient grounds for an assertion. There is some message in his autobiographical sketch of the childhood roots of an ethical-philosophical spirit, a message intended for use by A. He makes clear about himself the intimate and dominant relationship to a father in the development of character. He unites the father with a knowledge of grammatical rules. He makes himself the paradigm of these rules. By law, the exception is identified. Everyone is an exception in some way or another to the universality of selfhood. Every personality, embodying the freedom to become, is also a unique experience of limitation. The inner intensity of personality is precisely the practice of limitation. Judge William practices a knowledge of self-limitation. He constantly translates himself from stage to stage, striving to overcome the disparity between fatherhood and father ideal. Like Oedipus, he constantly inquires after the father in himself; he is disturbed by his own authority. The paradox of the ethical, implied in b's autobiography and personal theories, is that one is always an exception to one's own notion of the commonly recognized universals, and yet one is the responsible authority whose actions make this paradox real. b becomes paradoxical but, as in the father-son relationship, he suppresses the conflict with seriousness and rational theories. He is attracted to the wistful antirational temperament of a kind of exceptional individual which he himself has never been. He presents himself as an ethical teacher, which he is, and a good one at that; and he makes himself father to a son in order to explore and reaffirm the sense of purpose which is the burden of his authority.

Who is the mother: a is the woman in childbirth, the mother to the father-to-be. b's own estrangement attracts him to the birth of personality from the primal self, signified by the integration of the will. He participates in his own ethical plight in that process, a participation that brings him closer to the father in himself—his own salvation. Through the education of subjectivity he gains a comrade with whom to share the burden of the ethical task, finding reaffirmation of his own situation by practicing self-limitation. It is love that impells b, a love that, like his own father's, conceals itself in an imperative, "Chose yourself."

The ethical educator who makes the total being of the other his concern is an educator of consciousness: he seeks to aid a transformation at the very ground of experience and valuation. Transforming a wholeness requires the wholeness of the educator's presence in that event. The theoretically transforming event, B's letter, reveals such an educational character. He engages the full range of ethical virtuosity in a contest with the aesthetical individual's enthusiasm and self-love. If B could reunite himself with an ethical A, he would simultaneously have reunited the father and son in himself. This is the erotic element in the ethical procession of becoming: the romance of separation and reunification, and the energy subsequently released. The educational erotic is a well-kept secret. It had to be discovered in a secret compartment of an old bureau purchased from an antique dealer, it is that ancient.

The renewal of self, actualized and substantiated in personality, moves through the teleological circle: from oneself through the world to oneself again. Return, repetition, and development give this movement its historical qualities. Does B return vicariously to a former self-identity in his relationship to A? Is the teleological nature of his educating the rediscovery of a previous transformation of self? Clearly, he has never been like A. More probably he is attracted to a kind of person whose experience has been quite different from his own. He perceives an "immanent teleology" in A's life and symptoms (melancholy, despair, dread); he holds to the transcendent factors in his own life, prematurely resolving back the conflict of faith into the realm of ethical harmony and balance, subordinating his own paradoxical predicament (the noble exception) to a rule of reason (the righteous rationality).

It does not seem as though B's ethical life will prove satisfactory to A's condition. Nor would A's rebirth resolve B's struggle. They might be helpful to one another. But, for all his insight, B misjudges A's character. Had B read A's literary

productions he would have realized that A is not ignorant of
the incommensurability of the real and ideal in life. He has
his own equivalent understanding of limitation. Not from
vanity but in preponderance of actuality has A become an
ironist. A dwells in the aesthetic realm because he is persistently fascinated by a conception of himself as a locus and
result of unknown, determining powers. His notion of freedom is to experience himself as a wholly unique complexus of
effects. But he is not innocent of the contradictions that constitute daily experience. It is precisely the limitations individuality encounters that A recognizes and experiences; these
make him the ironist and author of tragicomic essays. For
this poet's sensibility, immediacy is already lost in the penetration of self-illusion. The power of irony is his way through
to his own authentic ground.

Judge William does not seem to recognize the full power of
the literary ironist, A. Or, when he does, it appears to be
understood as A's vanity rather than his concrete encounters
in life. The disintegrated dimension of pristine unity, the
ruins upon which the ironist builds his style, remains unrecognized in B's analysis. Putting this together with Judge William's own account of the solution to the problem of the individual's relationship to "first immediacy," one sees that the
abstract character of his call to repentance lacks a corresponding reality in relationship to A.

A seems to have come further in a concrete understanding
of life's many contradictions than B, while B has come further
to being the author of his own created life situations and the
maxims and moral principles that underlie them. The two
acquaintances do meet. The reader óf *Either/Or* has the
opportunity to continue to discover this event.

6.
Finding the Perfect Limit

If Judge William locates his capacity as an ethical-philosophical personage in the historical father-son relationship, the
aesthetically oriented individual, A, focuses his attention on
the female figure, and in particular the mother or daughter.
He personifies tragedy, in his essay "The Ancient Tragical
Motif as Reflected in the Modern," as a mother's love that
soothes the troubled child with infinite gentleness.[1] The
father-haunted B has his opposite in the mother-enchanted A.

In distinguishing the respective provinces of aesthetic and
ethical judgments, A draws up the following ratio: the strict
paternal is to the ethico-religious as the mild maternal is to
the aesthetic.[2] As the essay develops he intensifies the ratio,
putting the proportions thus: metaphysics is to ethical knowledge, on one side, and on the other side, the ratio is never
explicitly expressed but appears to be formulated as an unknown, X, relative to existence.[3] This unknown variable in
the logic of aesthetics, A embodies in Antigone. Antigone, as
primal figure for tragedy, especially tragedy pressed to its
modern limit, is the mythical daughter-sister. In the hands of
A she becomes transformed toward the confines of the aesthetic itself: she becomes *virgo mater*.[4] The enigmatic transformation of Antigone, from the ancient to the modern
through A's reinterpretation, alters the expression of the mys-

terious and powerful forces acting upon the individual.

A is devoted to experiencing himself as an unknown, a quality toward which sensuous factors gravitate forming multiple constellations of affect. The freedom to be everything is an infinite one and A, as a member of a secret society, the Symparanekromenoi (Fellowship of Buried Lives), strives to exercise his infinitude expressively rather than instrumentally—as B does in bringing about universal-man. B accuses A of practicing a literary style then in fashion, irony: a use of language which conveys an incongruity between what is stated and what is meant. The force of irony is to undermine the acceptable, the established, or so-called real world. B sees A's irony as an experimental attitude toward life, an uncommitted daemonic toying with other individuals through dissimulation and manipulation. When A slips the five dollar bill into the hands of a poorhouse woman whom he clandestinely overhears wishing to a friend for just such a gift of grace, he plays the daemonic experimentalist role.[5] Like some of his literary productions, A plays with the common notion of the expectable. B sees his actions as malevolently rather than benevolently motivated. There is evidence for this judgment, that A practices an essentially negative irony, and it would take a good defense attorney to free him from the charge. Such a defense might attempt to illustrate that the defendant also expresses himself through the style of a positive form of irony and that the one at least balances the effects of the other. It is this positive irony that Judge William neglects in his ethical case against aesthetically oriented A.

Antigone, the tragic heroine who occupies his predisposition, represents such a positive project of A's style. The apparent contradiction of a positive irony, by which it undermines the real in order to arrive at a deeper possibility of reality, expresses A's concern for his own infinitude, the unboundedness of his being. Content and form are mutually limiting components of expression. The adequacy of one to the other reveals the aesthetic perfection that the term beauty signifies. But, when the central content is an infinite self, in this case given by the figure of an eternal Antigone, the bounds of the formal requirement must themselves be transcended. A posits an almost impossible object, an Antigone who breaks the limits of the antique concept of tragedy. The expressive style through which A opens himself to the world requires a content that asserts its supremacy over the formal component, while doing that form justice. The irony of A is positive but paradoxical. It makes a conflict with expectation yield a higher truth. This higher truth, which B calls A's "higher madness," is the outcome of a rhetorical approach consistent with the rules of the Fellowship to which A belongs.

The female tragic figure, argues A, is a consistent device for arousing the empathy of his melancholic associates. This is all the more true if she can be given new life relevant to the modern situation. This relevancy requires certain literary measures in achieving its ideal. And these measures of relevance, if successful, provide the perfect limit through which the aesthetic essayist demonstrates his literary art, and his art of living—poetic infinitude.

The literary and life arts are codified as one by the little society, intrigued by the dark secretive side of experience. They call the "fragmentary style" one that is faithful to the constant newness of each moment, the aesthetic instant that "never actually becomes present, but always has an element of the past in it."[6] Their art is then lying grammatically in the imperfect, the conditional, such that every poetic production remains essentially a posthumous one. The poetics to which A adheres, views the poetic personality as always ahead of or beyond its literary effort. The poet's existence is not futurally related to his work; his presence is above rather than before or after the work he has bequeathed and left behind him.

The goals of the Symparanekromenoi are curiously similar to the ethical intentions evinced by B's letter. At every meeting of the Fellowship a "renewal and rebirth" is called forth. But unlike B's criteria, the poetics of the Fellowship depends upon a reinterpretation of its own unchanged productivity. A finished work is therefore to be avoided, just as a finished personality is abhorred. An aesthetic production and one's personality are conceived romantically as a content that never allows itself to be bordered by completeness, concept, or finality. The poetic irony of the society performs a "gleaming transitoriness," a lightning illumination.[7] The poet's infinitude outleaps the time and space of the work. The positiveness, characterized by A's essay on tragedy, is the "more than what appears to be" sense that the author gives his words. Indeed, he is more than what he appears to be and is renewed and reborn through every artistic event; though how he does this is a secret, concealed in accordance with the sacred customs and rules of the society.

A explicitly describes the poetics of the Fellowship, an act that could be seen as self-contradictory to the intrinsic values of a stylistic code that strives to appear accidental and careless. But even here his postulates are only negative: to avoid closely coherent works, to avoid wholes, never to see an idea through to its conclusion, and so on. The artistic touch is meant only to give an impression of rebelliousness and give the authorship a revolutionary image, an impression that is itself a further deception. Therefore, the reader is again placed in the interpretive posture that seeks to uncover a secret: the riddle of a perfect limit.

Death is the answer to the riddle of limit. A's account of a modern Antigone, toward which the entire essay builds, breaks the conventional formal requirements of the tragical. The modern Antigone's death is an ambiguously caused suicide resulting from a life-annulling collision of a secret memory with a hopeless, unfulfillable future life. In his dramatic development of the character, A internalizes the classical Antigone's situation and produces a character who turns ultimately into an all-encompassing emotion. The daughter of Oedipus becomes the bride of sorrow and her devotion to his secret fate makes her the mother of the tragic mood itself.

Unlike the classical tragedy, Creon does not put Antigone into a subterranean cave; she willfully enters the subterranean world of reflected sorrow and anxiety, she enters a secret self and draws A and his listeners with him down into the spiritual death of evenly matched colliding forces. Antigone's death is an infinitude; the drama inwardly perpetuates itself and rather than drawing to a conclusion, her death becomes immortal, transforming and transubstantiating the objective substantive forces (which give the ancient Antigone an element of innocence) by taking them over in the form of a spiritual guilt. By making absolute the relative guilt of classical Antigone—a relativity composed of the individual's deeds and the laws of family, race, and state—an almost Christian figure emerges from the Greek myth and the aesthetic category of tragedy comes to balance precariously on the edge of religious experience.

Everything in the essay serves to intensify this precarious balance. Poetic irony is not only illustrated by the all-but-invisible Antigone, but the procedure by which she is created shows A to be busily undermining the fortress of traditional aesthetic categories. Disguised as a scholar trying to distinguish the ancient and modern conceptions of tragedy, A begins by showing that the student of tragedy is immediately limited by the fact that his interpretation already presupposes and relies upon a knowledge of tragedy handed down through the ages. The individual needs the experience of the tragic itself in order to interpret likeness and difference in the ancient and modern forms. The historical-conceptual view limits the scholar's ability and conditions his insight into tragedy.[8] A eliminates the possibility that anyone could draw absolute differences between classical and modern tragedy. No one can place himself outside of a historical perspective to note such distinctions. What A implies, in his first ironical move, is that we are already involved with a sense of the tragic; it is not only a dramatic category but a condition of mankind. Positive irony works in this way, that mutually exclusive but related terms are brought to their proximal limits at which point some new inner aspect comes to light. Whatever interrelates the new and the old forms, it is more than mere nominalism and less etherial than idealism, it is in the experience of the existing individual himself.

There is a second advance on the study of tragedy undertaken by the scholarly A. Making the conventional move of recalling Aristotle's treatise in the *Poetics*, he contradistinguishes tragedy from comedy. Tragedy concerns itself with thought and character as a means of action, the plot is primary to the individuality of the characters. With classical comedy, character and situation are made primary and the plot revolves around individual action rather than external cosmic forces. The purpose of comedy is the arousal of laughter, the ridiculous, but the comical changes with time from one generation to another. Hence, there is a "high degree of variability relative to the different conceptions of the ridiculous entertained in the world of consciousness."[9] Could this variable ever be such that what produced laughter in one age produces tears in another? A opens his essay up to the possibility for alloying laughter and tears, the tragicomic motif.

A declares that his effort is to show that ancient tragedy is embodied within the modern. Is one the limit of the other? The topic allows A the opportunity to turn a polemic against what he considers the comic-oriented disposition of his epoch. The modern individual no longer experiences the nature of cosmic limits. This is due to the fact that he looks in the wrong place. The tragic factor is no longer in the external world; it is individualized and, like comedy, lies in the inner man. The modern comedy only hides a deeper tragedy and A offers to uncover the internal cosmology. He begins with two brief examples of his wit: social movements seeking to counteract human isolation end up reinforcing the isolation of individuals by emphasizing the mass; and the many associations of the time prove, through overcompensation, the disorganization of the age. By exaggerating the relative, the inner paradoxical comes to light.

A's essay is a study in extremes. Guilt and innocence, action and passivity, individual will and cosmic law (fate) provide the framework of the tragic collision. According to his own analysis, the emphasis on individuality in the modern age reveals a similarity between modern tragedy and ancient comedy. The true tragic quality has been forgotten due to the loss of belief in mythical forces and destined lives. Repeatedly, the modern tragic hero becomes comical in asserting his individuality against the laws of necessity. The absolute, like the solemnity of mortal authority, has weakened. Modern tragedy, says A, has neither epic foreground nor background, neither past nor future—"the hero stands or falls on his own action."[10] Clearly, and ironically, A implies that the tragedy of the modern age lies in its very conception of tragedy as action subject to individualistic resolution and judged not by gods or through the symbols of higher forces but in terms of ethical categories, good and evil. The aesthetical ambiguity has been lost: the hero is either guilty or innocent, either active or passive, in these nineteenth century dramas. Moral righteousness replaces the ecstatic experience of the beautiful juxtaposition of elements in conflict. Life is reduced to the middle-ground view of a popular notion of happiness. Ultimately there is neither tragic destiny nor religious salvation. What then is humanity, asks A, without "either the sadness of the tragic, or the profound sorrow and profound joy of the religious?"[11] Both the tragic and the religious immediacy have collapsed. A's effort is to restore tragedy to its modern relevance.

In seeking the perfect limit for the conditions of new tragedy, A first formulates the requirement that both innocence and guilt must be retained, hence the ancient in the modern, but that they need deepening and intensification rather than resolution in the direction of the one or the other. An individual in whom guilt and innocence are made absolute combines the elements of Christian guilt-consciousness and the ancient mythical consciousness of innocence before the gods. Such a character is a historical impossibility, but A's initial formulation sets its aim upon this impossible personality. Inadvertently, he discovers that the model of these combined absolutes is united in the life of Christ. Action and suffering, freedom and obedience are viewed as absolute and identical by A. Apparently, he has again stumbled beyond the domain of aesthetics in following the consequences of his new tragedy. Recoiling from this pathway, A regains his balance by noting that the depiction of Christ crucified belongs essentially to the realm of metaphysics. He reestablishes his proportions and ratios, realizing that this model for the tragic character would have led to a conception of remorse and a condition requiring nothing less than repentance to resolve the situation. "Remorse has a sacredness which obscures the aesthetic, it may not be seen, least of all by the spectator, and it requires a different kind of self-activity."[12]

The consequences of the absolute must be avoided if the aesthetic jurisdiction is to be retained. Aesthetic ambiguity, by which the tragical remains dramatically effective, is arrived at through the relativity of sorrow and guilt, where sorrow is what *happens to* the individual and guilt is how the individual finds himself *responsible for* and to it. A new category of the tragic is therefore made relevant to the modern situation: anxiety.

Tragic sorrow involves the experience of forces lying outside one's control; tragic pain denotes a reflected suffering where the individual's plight is also self-caused. The perfect limit brings the inner and outer powers into equilibrium. This is the case with A's Antigone. Antigone experiences anxiety, an ambivalence of attraction and repulsion in relation to her father's double crime (killing the father, marrying the mother). She is the only person who knows this secret, and whether her father Oedipus knew it remains uncertain. She inherits his sin while bearing her love for Oedipus—continuing the tragic incest, which weds her to Oedipus's secret life. She possesses her guilt in the form of knowledge, but she is also innocent to the degree that the deeds she makes herself responsible for and carries with her are inherited. The story is further complicated by Antigone's love for a young man, whose love for her makes a double collision. The first tragic opposition arises between Antigone's love for her father (she is the model daughter) and for herself. Her self-love would not be too great a sacrifice. But now the intensity is increased, she must sacrifice the passion of her beloved as well. Now she cannot tell her secret for her beloved's sake, yet he perceives Antigone's reserve with even greater passion believing that whatever difficulties are being disguised they are not insurmountable to him. The qualities of the modern Antigone are "unrest in her sorrow, ambiguity in her pain," a sympathetic and passionate double collision.[13]

Reflection on her situation only reveals to Antigone the impossibility of a resolution. She loves and fears her father's memory. The entire Greek drama is internalized by the character: her fate is historical (heredity), her sorrow is made painful, anxiety replaces fear, and a secret knowledge occupies the place of an ancient riddle.

Antigone is responsible and faithful to her father's memory, and her enforced silent secret becomes an idea of holiness to her. She is transformed by this idea, devoted to it, and her vow is a marriage to a remembrance. The action of the classical tragedy occurs in the time of the mythical present. A's Antigone has her action behind and ahead, in past and future, in memory and expectation.

A's version modernizes the Antigone by placing greater emphasis upon the guilt experience than upon innocence. The modern man, and especially the wounded natures of the Symparanekromenoi, are attracted by and their compassion is aroused by the portrayal of guilt as destined. Antigone's guilt remains within the aesthetic in one sense, that it is universal and relative to the accident of fate; her guilt is heredity, and in it a parallel to the guilt of the race is offered. Innocence is present to make the guilt of A's Antigone aesthetically ambiguous and to give the character a modern ambivalence expressed by anxiety. She takes the external accidental factors into herself. Her actions become inwardly directed, just as her sorrow is reflective. Antigone is no longer a character. By the end of A's reading Antigone is gone, vanished into the pure total mood that is A himself. There is no outward drama; Antigone is impossible to perform outside the essay because no action is reflected from her. She has reached a limit, the limit of action itself. Antigone etherializes and modern man is born. Her suicidal death brings A and the Fellowship to life.

The perfect limit for A is a total mood without an object; it is the pure emotional state in which all finite claims are withdrawn. The world becomes a single emotion, and the individual an embrace. Reality is sacrificed for a purely possible self: that is the irony of poetic infinitude.

A models his aesthetic fascination around the image of a tragic heroine. It is also his secret that she carries, that the tragic action has already occurred. It is the incestuous relationship that preoccupies A's imagination, and his Antigone's votive love for Oedipus perpetuates the cycle. Every passion has its dialectic, says A.[14] He conceives his heroine as both virgin and mother. In his fantasy A is carried along by the character he seeks to create. He describes Antigone as the woman with whom he has "rested in a night of love, as if she had entrusted me with the deep secret, breathed it and her soul out in my embrace."[15] The embrace of language brings Antigone into A's possession. The trace that spiritualized Antigone leaves behind is a mood of enchantment: A's love for a mother figure pregnant with himself, a melancholic version of immortality as uncreatedness.

Metaphysics is to ethical knowledge as Antigone is to existence: a transcendent limit, an infinite possibility, an ecstasy, an irony.

The perfect limit is a paradoxical principle the expression of which is finite and imperfect in relationship to the infinitude of its poetical contents. A faces the problem of the limitations of speech through a double irony—his tragic mime becomes itself a jest. Seeing himself in his own comic situation, A advances to the edge of an aesthetical concern, just as B has moved to the edge of an ethical predicament.

Viewed as a kind of footnote to the essay on tragedy, A's "Rotation Method" gives the impression that the contradictory nature of a perfect limit has itself become mastered through literary poetic expression. He makes limit itself a method to the attainment of poetic infinitude. It is not the content of self that needs rebirth, but one's interpretation of that content can be varied in poetic delivery. The poet is like the man who cultivates the soil: he depends upon a rotation of crops and fallowing of fields to maintain its productivity.

> Here we have at once the principle of limitation, the only saving principle in the world. The more you limit your-self, the more fertile you become in invention.[16]

To rotate (*veksel*) is to turn about a central axis. The saving principle of this circular movement, in A's essay, is the fertility of self through the control of remembering and forgetting. Entanglement and commitment that threaten the ability to control one's memory and expectations are to be avoided. A permanent occupation, friendship, marriage, and all forms of admiration are held at a distance. The individual, says A, must identify his arbitrariness with the accidental in the external world.[17]

The upper limit of the interesting is boredom. The individual can remain within the eternally variable category of the interesting by constantly changing the temporal structure, by practicing an art of remembrance and forgetfulness. The poetics of temporality brings A into the Augustinian paradox in which forgetting is placed under the domain of remembering. When forgetting is understood as a capacity subject to willful action, (i.e., is made voluntary), the self as a controlling agent becomes dubious, the familiar temporal world takes on a strangeness. The last standpoint of poetic irony is the confrontation with its own sense of time. A's essay gives the impression that the poet has won a victory over the temporal limit, if only by having characterized and outleaped the confrontation between irony and existence, positing himself outside every definitive element, every limit.

Where B has perceived the structure of reason in the objective world, through the subjective eyes of the mind's trust in reason, A discovers the accidental through the perceptive disposition of an arbitrary self. In his hands the self becomes a fiction and the poet its ever changing author.

7.

Educating Consciousness at a Limit

There is no easy access to the poet, who bears himself backward into the womb of the mythical mother, or is carried by the spirit of Mnemosyne into multiple worlds of newly conceived selves; for whom human limit becomes a literary tool and every "other" is a potential *alazon*. B, the straight man, but with enough of the *eiron* in him to make the struggle dramatic, advances into the kingdom of the beautiful, bearing the shield of *summum bonum* (highest good) and equipped with the spear of a moral imperative, "Choose yourself." Because A and B dwell in incongruous temporal modes, the ethical squire must first transfix A (the author of fictive selves) at a particular moment and in a particular stage of development in order that his message finds its mark. Either/or becomes the grammatical principle of transformations where one realm is brought into relationship with another. B listens for the sigh of melancholy indicating the interim between ironical movements and, by focusing upon the / of either/or, he drives the wedge of finitude which separates, while inexorably joining together, two sides of every fundamental life proposition. B's effort is to enclose the aesthetical within the kingdom of the ethical and, by doing so, to hold A fast at a limit.

The logico-grammatical disjunctive either/or sets a boundary between two related statements where the truth of one statement means the falsehood of the other. According to Judge William, he who stands in the moment of decision confronts himself with an either/or. The individual, constantly faced with the opportunity to act decisively, brings himself to full presence through a temporal determination, an exercising of the capacity to make things real, the moral will. He who chooses decisively, affirms his basic freedom to act within limits and to relate himself absolutely to the object of choice. When an individual makes himself the object of choice by wholly affirming his condition, then that individual legislates his independence. Such an autonomy has the principle of universality as ground of action. The individual self-legislator, the ethical man, asserts his freedom as comprehensive of personality, and his ability to decide for himself links him to a commonly shared intelligible world, the universal-human.

If the universal-human bears a resemblance to Kant's kingdom of ends it is certainly not by accident, since B appears to utilize the main thrust of thought in Kant's ethics. By a "kingdom of ends" Kant understood "the linking of different rational beings by a system of common laws."[1] As one of the formulas stemming from his categorical imperative Kant called mankind to become member and sovereign of such an ideal kingdom by invoking the command, "So act as if you were always, through your maxims, a lawmaking member in a universal kingdom of ends."[2] The progress toward this possible kingdom could be actually realized if the individuals made the maxims of their subjective interests conform to the rule prescribed by the categorical imperative, that acts of will be subject to the requirement that they hold without contradiction when formulated as universally applicable moral laws. But Kant recognized what B similarly echoes in his letters to A, that the universality of moral will requires that the individual free himself from the dominations of "sensuous attachments." There is a faculty of "inner freedom," report Kant and B accordantly, which enables the individual to release himself from the domination of inclinations. This power of independence gives a man the feeling for the worth of self and serves as compensation for the sacrifices called up by duty.[3] This mastery, brought about by duty and reverence for law, marks the rebirth of the person into the true life of self. The condition that coincides with this rebirth is "self-contentment," where the self-contentment of mortals is a parallel experience and analogy to the self-sufficiency that can be ascribed to a Supreme Being.[4] By means of the form of his imperative, Kant derives a conception of perfection as the complete accordance of will and feeling with the moral law. Though such a perfect virtue is commanded by reason in its practical use, it is not fully attainable by human beings at any given moment. Kant calls this perfect moral will "holiness," and he arrives at a notion of the divine as a limit-idea toward which human beings strive as an ideal state. The indefinite, unending progress toward this ideal calls upon the faith of the individual in the very process, revealing an understanding that all duties are divine commands guiding man from lower to higher stages of moral perfection.

Judge William, likewise, appears to derive his notion of the Absolute from his apprehension of the universal-human. In his eyes duty is the inward requirement of an individual's authenticity, a sign that reveals to him that he is "correctly oriented" in life. The apprehension of duty leads the individual to recognize that a greater context, a broader structure of reason, surrounds and resonates his actions. This coherent reality, to which the intelligibility of his actions leads him, is represented in absolute terms, the greatest of which is the divine presence, God. Concurrently, B discovers that no individual ever attains the perfect identity with the ideal universal-human, that each one is in some way an exception to the universality of the common good and that, therefore, each individual becomes "extraordinary" or an "exception" in relationship to his own formulation of the universal fullness that lies before him.

Judge William departs from the Kantian formulation of the harmonious self-contentment within the rational limits of the practical will when he opens his description of the reality of despair and the remorse that seeks a transcendent principle to overcome the experience of imperfection. The rift in the human domain of finite freedom reveals a self-alienation between the individual self and the self's own conception of its perfection. Consequently, the individual discovers a separation between himself and the representation of the Absolute. A certain discontinuity arises in the coherency of the universal, a certain incongruity shows itself through the fabric of reason causing a man to sorrow over his remoteness from the kingdom of perfection and to experience anxiety over the restrictions of his own nature—the narrowing of existence.

Unlike Kant, b's discourse carries him over to the theological. The two kingdoms, that of the finite and the infinite, lack a uniting principle. Since the finite side has reached a limit, only an act coming from the side of the infinite can further the individual to his rebirth. The attitude of repentance serves to guide the individual back to his origin in God. There, in that atonement, he would receive God's grace and be reborn. Repentance functions within an immanent dialectic, a willfully animated logic, through which limitation leads to an inner intensity, a passion that reveals the deeper meaning of the individual's common plight—a realization which resolves him back into harmony with himself and the cosmos.

b's narrative of the meaning of either/or enables him to derive a role in relationship to that meaning, a role that itself helps him to resolve the incongruities of finite and infinite freedom. His response to a's fictive selves is the autobiographical account he builds toward through the biographical account of historical personalities on the way to the ethical. Again, in this approach, he is apparently following the advice Kant gives in his "Methodology," that access to the moral will of another can be gained through the use of historical characters whose embodiment of virtue produces veneration in the pupil.[5] Hence, b describes various Greek personages, the Roman Nero, and a sequence of modern characters, e.g., the count and countess, "poor Ludvig Blackfeldt," the mystic, to name several. But all these biographies serve to illustrate some incomplete resolution of the problem of ethics and rebirth. He uses his own biography to illustrate the positive in ethical life, and his own writing to affirm life from the side of the reborn. This variation on the Kantian approach is consistent with the entire procedure of conjoining sides of personality. For, just as the task of the student is to have intercourse with himself, it is the goal of B to be rejoined with A under the category of friendship. He adds to the Kantian paradigm a developmental and historical dimension in the relation between student and teacher, and B's personalized ethics brings the status of the moral educator into question with the final paradox—inability to achieve the universal-human in spite of good will and adequate intelligence.

A's essay and lecture on tragedy can be seen as a response to B's ethical offering, assuming that the letter and the lecture are concurrent. He rejects the requirement of the ethical imperative to choose oneself absolutely. He seems to have already perceived the consequences of individual limit and sets out instead to seek for the poet's infinitude, an ironical relationship to the real, the common, the expected.

Poetic irony tries to take advantage of the contradictions it has encountered; it strives to make them its own content and to master them through a unifying form. The perfect accordance of form and content signifies a resolution of differences between self and world, and a victory for the poet. The poet, A, lets language give the appearance, through images, that paradoxicality results in the beautiful and serves the purposes of the work of art. The poetics of irony means that the subject, the author, transcends the paradox of finitude through the perfection of form and content and seems to hover masterfully over his work. A's essays seem to release their author, the inner speaker, from the limitations they discuss and express: historical conditioning, formal requirements, death, anxiety, boredom, among others. In this way, poetic irony exemplified by A shows the voice of the narrator moving beyond the circle of his speaking, leaving behind the contraditions and incommensurabilities that his language embodies. The only remaining difficulty for the poet-ironist is the interim between victories over life paradoxes. Because the ironist, like the thief, likes to or is compelled to return to the scene of the transgression, enough energy is necessitated to repeat this act—in this case, the annihilation of actuality—an infinite number of times. The poetic effort constantly seeks to renew itself, but a doubt arises in the ironist as to whether it is the freedom he gains through irony or the paradoxical nature of existence which compels him to persist.

Irony confronts the exclusive determinations of an either/ or in the same way it confronts all other contradictions, only this time it is the law of contradiction itself which it confronts. The poet, A, tries to take advantage of the either/or, turning it to his own purpose. Irony, true to the poet, seduces the either/or by accepting its claim and by emphasizing these claims to such an extent that they go over into their opposites, namely, neither/nor. A makes either/or seem to imply a difficulty with choice so great that it rises beyond human comprehension and capability; either/or signifies impossibility of true choice and yields only the consequences of regret for submitting oneself to its rule. "Do it or do not do it, you will regret both," says A. Whenever the individual situates himself in an occasion of absolute difference he exposes himself to the dialectic of choice and regret. The dialectic of expectation and disappointment is to be avoided through the realization that either/or signifies the realm of higher illusions—subject matter for the poetic irony.

A and B uncover transcendent principles in their confrontation with limitation. B finds repentance and historical consciousness at the far edge of universal human will; these principles enable him to resolve human limitation through forgiveness and continuity. A pursues acceptance from the gods, seeks the perfect state of being, and follows aesthetical categories to their polar extremities. He makes a literary form, irony, an all-pervasive attitude and an omnipresence in literary production which tries to burst the confines of the conventional and the finite. Irony becomes the vehicle of poetic infinitude, undermining the resistances of the real, sacrificing actuality for the pure realm of higher possibility—exercising the complete mutability of self, fictionalizing of personality, and an ecstasy of objectless emotion.

Neither A nor B passes through the portal their principles of transcendence open. B's notion of repentance founders upon a psychological limit: the remembrance of his mortal father, which he has incorporated into himself as the very origin of ethical law and reverence, becomes an interpretive opaqueness to the religious experience he seeks and otherwise transparently discovers. B satisfies himself with a sense of universality, a sense of common plight, of the guilt of mankind; his repentent attitude is generalized so that he receives a generalized rebirth, a generalized forgiveness. He seeks to share that sense of universality with A, the solitary, isolated individual devoted to immediacy. Educator William has the virtue of practicing his own limitedness as a principle of self-knowledge. He is almost successful. But he falls short at last: a concealed love and a pride in human limit itself distorts his effort and reveals his rationalized religiosity. A, on the verge of tragic limits, himself a kind of educator as essayist and lecturer, disdains the righteous rationality of B. He pursues the infinitude of a pure all-encompassing feeling for which his irony clears a space. A can never enter into that cleared space; his irony must be maintained, he must continue to hover above the clearing, pointing to it but never able to belong in the place that becomes temporal and hence limited the moment he descends to it. He seeks comfort in the mother-love of tragic destiny and is borne back toward a preexistent eternity that he never quite seems to reach.

Limit becomes threshold in the world of A and B. Each is at the threshold of his own consciousness, peering through the structure of ground and transcendence, the lower and higher demarcations which form the doorway of the self and the domain of being. And each views the other's realm as insufficient, as a building without a solid foundation, or as a solid foundation without a building; as a height without a corresponding depth, a depth without a height.

The heights and depths of consciousness in the world of A and B are like obliquely intersecting lines: the sublime and subliminal motifs of each of their lives converge at an apex. Whether the lines meet and end, or whether they cross and continue their individual directions is a question left open to the reader.

B apparently feels it necessary to call in another opinion to conclude the long argument, and sends A a final document as a sort of postscript, which the editor, Victor Eremita, assigns to the last section of *Either/Or*, the "Ultimatum." The arts of the letter, the essay, the aphorism, and the lecture have been employed. The form of the sermon with its prayer, gospel, and interpretation remains for the reader's consideration.

The sermon's author is an older friend of B, a parson assigned to a country parish on the Jutland heath. A new voice, that of an older man, perhaps more advanced in his wisdom than B, may at the last be able to evoke the life of the spirit that has now faded from the other "flowers of expression." Judge William approves wholeheartedly the message contained by the sermon; he believes that it expresses what he had meant to say and also what he would like to have been able to articulate. He has taken the words of the sermon to heart and advises A to do the same, to "think of yourself."

The parson's sermon, appropriately, concerns the question of that which edifies, that which promotes spiritual improvement. He begins with a reading of the gospel of St. Luke (19:41) in which Christ tells of the coming destruction of Jerusalem. Parson C advances his homily through a series of rhetorical questions which he sees reflected in the text: shall the righteous suffer with the unrighteous, does Divine reason not single out the innocent from the guilty, should good deeds go unrewarded? When we experience our actions as good deeds that deserve the promised rewards, we seek, says the parson, to prove ourselves as in the right before God.

Such an attitude presumes to contend with God, and is therefore lacking in that activity that makes for edification.

What then is edification for the individual? Parson c's sermon opens new ground in the narrative of educating consciousness, a ground that perhaps penetrates deeper than b's ethical reflections, shaking the very rational framework of the moral act; it may even soar higher than A's ecstatic feeling through its uplifting considerations of a paradox of love. Parson c calls into question the very nature of the motives that impell the teacher and the learner, the motives of self-improvement and self-knowledge. It is perhaps not strange that b sends a sermon to A which describes a love transcending the love that rewards righteousness and punishes wrongdoing, a love that has the capacity to experience itself as "in the wrong."

The parson continues rhetorically. Under what circumstances is it both more painful and more uplifting to be in the wrong? Is it not before the beloved that one wishes rather to be in the wrong than to be righteously sorrowing over the other's actions toward oneself? When love is present, it is preferable to be in the wrong than to have won a rightful position over against the beloved; and the expression for this wish to be in the wrong is an infinite relationship.[6]

The individual who is motivated by a will to be ever more right, and is continually seeking for the state of perfect rightness, commits himself to a self-enclosing, self-restraining process. The implications of the country parson's sermon, especially following upon b's long epistle, is that a moral will animated by the desire for complete rightness before all else is a desire animated by pride. Pride denies the givenness of its ability to pursue truth and truth of self. The virtuous individual can easily become proud, particularly if some injury lies concealed beneath the surface of virtuousness. Pride denies the fundamental givenness of the right to seek truth and goodness, for pride denies the freedom of the individual to first be in the wrong. Self-education that is animated by pride denies the ground of freedom and rejects its own givenness to seek. The betterment it reaches is an uncaring and finite increase of self, a love of self which, because it intensifies its defensiveness, becomes more painful. Parson c's sermon begins to speak to the offended consciousness which stands at its limit.

But how can one will to be in the wrong? Is this not a paradox in which one tries to give oneself that which is already given—humility, mortality? Parson c begins to approach this problem by drawing a careful distinction. In the relationship between the individual and God, the rational man might be willing to admit that he is in a state of error relative to the divine knowledge. He might be convinced of this state of error as a logical consequence of thought, derived as it were from the necessity of the concepts divine/mortal, perfect/imperfect. A rational knowledge compelling the individual to realize his limitedness and relative wrongness still presumes to control the fundamental fact, making itself superior in its own inferiority. In relation to God, continues Parson c, one must wish (rather than will) to apprehend oneself as in the wrong as an act of love stemming from God's absolute love. It is the modality through which the moment of receptiveness is reached, which essentially determines the infinite and edifying relationship.[7]

The confirmation of the freedom to be able to allow oneself to be in the wrong, grounds that which edifies. Neither the necessity of being wrong nor the pride of being right yields the infinite relationship that is edifying, that builds up and goes deep at the same time in one self. It is possible, adds the parson, that one may even be unfaithful to one's duty in response to the higher freedom which foregoes rightness and honor. His meditations verge on the reflections of Job (40:2). He does not resolve the consequences, nor does he deny the voice inside which asks whether things might not be otherwise, the insistent resistance of the self's claim to be right; rather, he encourages the intensity of the questioning of the law, the "deep inward movement" by which knowledge of the mind and the emotion of the heart reach the conviction that unites them in appropriation and belonging to the truth that edifies.[8]

Parson c's sermon describes the ultimate collision that A's vanishing tragic heroine fails to achieve and B's ethical principle covers over: the thought that discovers itself limited in its seeking and which lets that limit open itself to receive the unthinkable, the spontaneous acknowledgement of freedom as already given. The will impels reason to a point of unwilling resistance—that it is in need. To be in the wrong, by one's own wish, is to be needful. And needfulness awakens the nearness of what is sought. Need lies outside will and fantasy and the individual is outside his freedom when freedom, like rightness, is perceived as something to achieve, something to conquer. In his wrongness the individual lets himself be found out by that which he seeks, his ultimate. There, in the wrong, says Parson c, is the individual's perfection.

A makes an effort to lose himself in his tragic heroine or to delete himself in his irony. B calls for a finding oneself through giving birth to a second self; he comes closer to the goal of renewal through the thought that only by revealing oneself does one prepare receptively. But, when he might have been found, he hides in morality and the harmony of universality. The edifying sermon introduces an educative insight by clarifying the process of seeking, and by purifying the approach so that the seeker can be found in his seeking.

Consciousness cannot completely penetrate itself whether by fantasy or will. But by reaching a knowledge of its own confines, the individual self sees itself as looking out from within a place of being. From within, it comes nearer to its freedom—its freedom that is already given. The collision seems to be the requirement for presence to self, as if the self needed to be surprised by its own discovery: being found.

The papers of A and the letters of B are found, edited, entitled, and published seven years later by an individual who calls himself Victor Eremita. The public suspects that Victor is himself the author of the two volumes, since the literary device, discovering secret papers by unknown authors, has a certain popular romantic flavor making credible the notion of a philosophical work in novelistic form written under pseudonym. If this turns out to be the case, that the whole work has one author and that the author is himself disguised so that there seems to be a puzzle of authors within authors, then how should this mystification be understood—a mystification by one who appears to be outside the situation of a collision between extreme modes of life?

The author is apparently beyond the limits that his characters profile. Their discord has no resolve. Only the edifying sermon seems to reach a conclusion: "for only the truth that edifies is truth for you." Nevertheless, the parson's words are rather a tiding that opens up the themes of B's dense discourse to the light of reflection than a final conclusion for the whole work. Their collision has then no result, and this is perhaps appropriate for characters who are in conflict with themselves at their inner limits; or, as the editor says at the outset, at the point where an incommensurability is discovered between the inner and outer life-forms.

If the work has no conclusion, at least it ends. Edification qualifies the ultimate lesson, and the ultimate truth is the individual's concern for that which is uplifting. The editor's final and perhaps only advice is that the reader find himself in closest proximity to the character whose words reach him most intimately and proceed from that point.

A general confusion and curiosity surround the publication of *Either/Or* and, as is often the case with a book whose truth is obliquely pointed toward, the authorship became of primary interest. After some interchange of views and a complaint from a certain *Magister Artium* that he had been mistakenly and repeatedly accused of the authorship, Victor Eremita bequeathed to the public one last message, to this effect: if the book had no author, and no actual title, neither should it have a real editor. Rather, the work should encompass its own indeterminateness and as a book should not stand in any definite relationship to some special reader. Further, the editor's name was no personal nominative, not a *proprium* for the editor but an *apellativum* for the reader who would make himself the work's "first reader." He, then, whose motivation activates the work will experience a moment when Eremita (hermit) is his proper name, since a serious contemplation makes one solitary; though, perhaps at a later moment, Victor (triumphant) will become his chosen title, nearing as he will a victorious understanding of the text.[9]

The present reader is certainly not victorious since he has allowed the deception, that there were two or three authors, to predominate throughout his interpretation, seeking all the while a nexus where the lives of A and B would open up to one another. This oblique intersection seemed forthcoming as the characters neared each other through expression of their experiences with principles of limitation and through the evolving story in which eros drew together the pathos of the one and the ethos of the other. The reader's serious contemplations, however, were not able to triumph; the dramatis personae remained isolated and the love between learner and teacher—where the will of the one sought to win the imagination of the other—foundered, only to be revived again and transformed into the agapic love of Parson C's sermon.

Even the good parson's words, edifying as they may be, only give enthusiastic assurance that the doubter's question, "Could it not all be otherwise?" if pursued persistently, would produce the self-appropriation of that which one already knew and already had repeatedly willed. The love of which the parson speaks brings the conflict with limit closer to a resolution, uncovering a new way of belonging to existence. Yet, this needful wish, however much it evokes a transcendent principle of finite freedom, echoes the kind of immanent dialectic which was encountered in B's discourse. A truly transcendent point of departure remains unclarified, though Parson C's sermon prepares edifyingly for such action. In developing his private relationship with God, and perhaps in discovering God's love for mankind, Parson C loses sight of his congregation as existing individuals. Rather, he pictures from the pulpit an "ideal listener." His religious idealism achieves a premature certainty which elevates credibility above faith. The new life, which в also introduced, once again breaks forth without breaking through.

Even this final effort, of wishing to see oneself as limited to a domain bordered by the divine, nevertheless holds on to a notion of self-consciousness which closes the circle of its own self-becoming, albeit with the grace of God. Victor Eremita's characters all refuse to give up their self-consciousness whether through the control of irony or even to the point of turning humility into a principle of self-closure. Though there appears to be an idea of stages developing toward an ultimate perfection, and though the ethical is characterized as inclusive of the aesthetical, and the religious subsequently follows the principle of concentricity by including both the aesthetic and ethical, still each character remains qualitatively separated from the perfection toward which he orients himself. If the author has made this understanding possible through the inconclusive and paradoxical limits of self-consciousness, that no stage is a solution and that from within a stage or life orientation the nearness of an ultimate concern is still experienced as or shown to be infinitely distant, then it is not the stages (as в once pointed out) but self-transformation, the movement from and toward a stage, which deserves the reader's primary attention.

The present reader has looked in vain, following the common error, for the "real" author. Now he concludes along with the editor that there is no author but only a sequence of silences into which the reader listens. The conventional designations of the terms aesthetic, ethical, and religious are here broadened and personified to the degree that they become allegorical in pointing beyond themselves, having become explicit and in a sense empty of further enrichment or nourishment. They seek and reach an end, or terminate in a silence that gives the impression that the entire development has been metaphorical, has only served to transfer the reader from point to point, thus evoking the movement of transformation which itself becomes the principle experience of a revealing education.

8.

Either/Or: An Eventful Education

A of *Either/Or* pursues the art of self-limitation in order to sustain poetic infinitude, fallowing and rotating fields of memory and avoiding repetitions of experience. Attempting to dwell in the immediacy of life, he seeks to explore every possible aspect of the sensuous. Judge William, A's "ethical" acquaintance, calls on him to relinquish his childish activity by giving birth to himself. B implies a transcendent principle that enables an individual to take part in a more permanent renewal of life. Principles of moral action allow one to participate in a larger unity of experience which includes forms of absolute commitment through which one would belong to that perfection, expressed by the term "universal-human." B's efforts to describe the process through which one passes in attaining universality, cause him to pause in consideration of his own life story. He intends to make himself a didactic example for A. But he must also admit that his own life terminates in a self-consciousness that keeps him outside the universal-human. Perhaps, concludes B, we are all "exceptions" to human perfection. Human powers of reason founder upon an apprehension of the infinite objective of a finite process. B is reconciled to his destiny but does not discover the pathway by which one is guided to the religious life. His anticipation of a realm beyond the ethical is expressed in the sermon he sends to A. Parson c's sermon terminates the second volume.

The disjunction that the title *Either/Or* indicates is not resolved through the lives of any of the characters. Even though Parson c replaces b's notion of an "absolute" that is immanent in life by introducing the unconditional love of God (and, hence, moving us to the religious sphere), his "only the truth that edifies is truth for you" serves more to introduce further tasks of inwardness than to complete the journey. The perfection of one's nature understood as personality is replaced by Parson c's orientation to a further process of interiorization through recognition of ultimate imperfection. The edifying truth is then one whose appropriation by an individual enables him to ascend to a higher, transcendently given criterion. The idea of human becoming points to a deeper source of self-development than an ethical imperative. It points to the primordial possibility of a gift of freedom which lies deeper than the human will, one that is posited through love. This reorients the individual toward a fundamental act of receptivity, "being found."

Neither the aesthetic, ethical, or religious dispositions implicated in *Either/Or*, nor the characters who portray them, attain a conclusive victory. Because they turn in upon themselves in an effort to reach self-sufficiency, their self-consciousness becomes a hindrance to the attainment of perfection. The power of moral will to ascend the ladder of perfection is itself challenged. b becomes aware of this. His efforts to enable a rebirth process in A reveal his own limits to enable himself to reach that "higher concentricity" in which knowing and being become identical. Because none of these life attitudes has the quality of finality, we are left with two fundamentally different ways of considering their unity. The one view suggests that particular individuals hold particular life attitudes, and that these attitudes can be placed in a progressive order moving from lesser to greater perfection of human possibility. The perspective of the ethicist is such that it possesses and transforms the content of the aesthetic. Presumably the religious does something similar with the ethical. But a second understanding, more appropriate to the incompleted lives of *Either/Or*'s characters, is that these life dispositions are all simultaneously present in each adult person as aspects of the self, aspects here personified as dramatic characters.

Without denying the real importance that choosing between the distinctive differences of life attitudes entails in a world of either/or's, we can imagine another way of grasping the reality of these attitudes besides viewing them as an inevitable progression of stages. Perhaps this will allow us to realize the unity of *Either/Or*'s diversity of styles, mood, temperament, and dramatic juxtaposition—that this literary unity points us toward a personal embodiment. To begin, let us notice that B speaks about the aesthetic, ethical, and religious as not only life views or attitudes (*livs-anskuelser*) but as stages (*stadier*) and as spheres (*sphaerer*). Each of these terms suggests a different conception of human becoming: life attitudes suggests perspectives on experience as well as the intimation of personal history of "life-time"; stages indicates linear sequences and perhaps hierarchy (a lower, a higher stage); and spheres brings to mind the idea of horizon, the spatiality of one's awareness (its extent) plus the duration or temporal sense in which a person dwells (qualities of intensity). Views, stages, and spheres do not seem to possess precise differentiation, yet it seems that B finds one term more appropriate than another in a given context; hence, "stages of the erotic," "the sphere of the philosopher's mediation," and "the drunken revelers and penny sportsmen's view of life."[1]

The various uses these terms serve indicate different ways of characterizing the person in history, where history, recalling B's use of that term, refers to "the choice of freedom" through which a person "produces himself" and gives to the transitory nature of life experience a continuity.[2] View, stage, and sphere are all metaphors for the individual's relation and orientation to time as inner history. Each manner of speaking is capable of emphasizing different factors of what we might call the spatio-temporal character of human becoming. But no single term adequately exhibits the whole of this elusive subject. It is of utmost importance that we examine the structures these metaphors of human becoming create in the context of *Either/Or*, where they are presented as characters and only secondarily as concepts, and where the contrast opened between them helps us to recognize what is at issue (how they make a difference) and how they function as interrelationships. Once we have grasped this we will be prepared for further developments in Kierkegaard's use of life dispositions which are here prefigured.

If we consult each of the characters themselves for how their expressive life might best be conceived, we find A dwelling primarily in the past but struggling, as for instance with his melancholy, not to allow memory to become static; we listen to B's exhortations to be in the moment of choice, to become present to oneself through decisive action; we follow Parson C's sermon with its emphasis on the joy of "being in the wrong before God" and the hope toward which this joy directs us. The past (memory), the present (choice), and the future (expectation, faith) correspond to the mental attitudes of these three character types of *Either/Or*. The aesthetic, ethical, and religious figures at one moment seem to stand distinctively apart from one another in the order of lower to higher; at another moment they can be taken together inclusively as concentric circles one within another; and still at another moment we grasp the interpenetrability of temporality as they become past, present, and future tenses of one's own existence, no longer determinable as beside-each-other but despatialized as intersecting temporal dimensions.

The incompleteness of these characters makes the linking of their lives possible. The concurrence of dispositions in *Either/Or* reflects the simultaneity of the whole person as a many-sided being constantly confronted by contrary forces and the need to integrate or choose among them. Our own interpretation of the drama of contrasting characters must resolve into a unified constellation of meaning the motifs of character development, rebirth, moral autonomy, historical consciousness, friendship, and, in general, the whole context of self-education and educative attitudes. It is as if we were looking at a painting whose perspective was so cleverly handled that the viewer could never quite extricate himself from the picture space in order to make a more distant and detached observation. Instead he is forced to work out the composition by proceeding further into its recesses.

The hypothesis we have begun to explore is that the characters of *Either/Or* constitute for the reader the dialectical nature of human becoming. That, reechoing B, from whose lips the very conception of life-history issues, "not the particular stage but the transition between stages," is of greatest importance. We are most aware of our own becoming and of our holding a value perspective when we experience resistance to development, alteration of assumptions, or transformations in life. This suggests that these dispositions, taken concurrently as multiple dimensions of the singular self, have the quality of temporal demarcation—that they exhibit the *eventfulness* of becoming historical to oneself through individuation. In the case of *Either/Or*, with its dramatic qualities of the novel form, what events take place? First there is the event of Victor Eremita discovering the papers of A and B. Second, there is the event of our reading what Victor has offered to us. But does anything happen in *Either/Or* in the way of action? The only happening is the extension of forms of address by the characters as they meet in the reader. The relationship of B in his letter to A does point to the event of educating where to educate means to be moved to assist another individual in altering his basic life disposition through some manner of facilitation. To educate reflects doubly the *movement* of transformation which calls forward the person seeking to bring another forth into his own possibilities, while it reflects the *motive* to educate that reveals the educator as also in a process of becoming. The following interpretive exploration is admittedly speculative extention of *Either/Or* as the eventful meeting of educator and pupil. Hopefully, we will be able to reconnect with Kierkegaard by carrying out our own form of double reflection.

The eventfulness of dispositions facing into one another begins with Judge William's turning toward A. And it is in the ethical disposition, similarly, that the idea of dispositions as interpretive life-attitudes—postures of becoming in personal history—first arises. This is because, first, the ethical itself marks a rebirth, the individual "producing himself" as a history which can then compare itself to a former state, and because there in the ethical temporal experience becomes teleological, the individual discovering himself as both process and goal of becoming.

Process and goal are dual aspects of human becoming in the relationship of means and ends. Process orientation and goal orientation should be interrelated and mutually consistent dimensions of the educative domain. But they are often separated from one another or conceived as polarities between which one must choose. So, for example, in the teaching of philosophy, we find the school of thought which emphasizes the "here and now" activity of self-knowledge conceived as personal growth, and, on the other hand, the school that emphasizes a knowledge of the subject matter as a reaching up to the standards of the tradition. This, of course, begs the question as to whether the here-and-now approach could lead to a knowledge of the traditional subject matter or whether knowledge of the tradition could lead to an activity of self-knowledge. Each aspect is really indispensable to the other, as we shall see.

In the relationship of educator to pupil, a conception of human becoming may be decisive in structuring the educative event. For example, if life development is conceived as a linear progression from stage to stage in the hierarchical order of ascent from lower to higher, educating becomes primarily a matter of the educator bringing the pupil up to his degree of competence and maturity. This conception is metaphorically spatial; stages of development are distributed as a sequence moving from lower positions to higher ones. The goal of such an educational undertaking is to reach toward the status of the educator, perhaps to the extent that the goal is the personality of the educator himself as source of authority. The educator helps by setting goals as standards of accomplishment to be reached. This spatial conception of education emphasizes the relative *positions* of educator and learner, i.e., the place and role they play in relationship to one another. Let us call this the "positional truth" of becoming given a goal orientation. And let us term an awareness that is so attuned a "positional consciousness."

Returning to *Either/Or*, the goal that Judge William sets for A is to choose himself, to gain moral autonomy in becoming part of William's "kingdom of ends." Nevertheless, the positional relationship of William (the morally superior) is undermined by William's own discourse. Although the ethical domain rests securely upon what appear to be historical-philosophical values, particularly from Kant and Hegel, and a kind of religious understanding, particularly Protestant, these traditional structures of value and interpretation become more uncertain by the end of B's second letter than at the beginning of his discourse. The effect of this uncertainty is the resultant impression that B has played out his competence as a moral superior and comes to stand alone on the edge of an abyss. The confrontation with limitation becomes a key dimension of B's understanding of himself as historical, as becoming individual. The dramatic effect of B's incomplete character alters the overall picture of *Either/Or*, and the assumption about life dispositions it contains. Just as B's series of "admirable" historical personages terminates in imperfection, the comparison of higher and lower selves dissolves into an eventful meeting of characters and their attitudes. The positional truth of an either/or education moves over into a *situational* one. The effect of *Either/Or* is to draw us into the potential meeting of characters and their becoming situationally interrelated. Another way to see this would be to say that the stages they portray become reflective within themselves; they become life situations and, when taken together, they comprise the many-sidedness of the educative event. We focus on the ethical educator, B, as at the center of this eventful education.

Why should we be drawn to the figure of B as the center of

an allegory of education? Is Judge William not a stuffy, out-
dated, moralistic, bourgeois, lower court civil servant, with
whom a decent modern and innovatively oriented educator
ought not to traffic? Simply in order to make a friend, he out-
steps the domain usually ascribed to the educator. He calls
for an intimacy, reveals himself in his limits, and throws his
whole person into the task of sacking A's aesthetic citadel.
The seriousness of his demeanor and position becomes something of a comic situation. It would have been customary to
portray such a man as Judge William as the figure of absolute
stability and authority, a figure whose position in life is un-
questionably respectful and secure. Instead, the Judge is
shown posed in the dilemma of his own life situation. Precisely the juxtaposition of positional and situational sides of
his character makes him relevant to contemporary issues in
education, as well as to the human sciences (counseling,
social work, therapy) in general.

Our hypothesis then is not only that *Either/Or* portrays a
sequence of life stages, each of which is qualitatively distinct
and, though concentrically related, stands in the positional
order of a hierarchy of values, but also that the disposition of
characters comprise aspects of the single self in dialectical
tension with itself. The whole to which the meeting of dispositions points, through the motif of educating one another, is
the simultaneity of these dispositions, which is the dimension
of depth reached in the story of the educative event. Our task
is not to choose one of them but to be their unity. Sequence,
goal, and position are emphasized as spatial conceptions of
the educative. We hear this in such familiar phrases as "upbringing," "being in a position to help," "reaching the mark."
But simultaneity, process, and situation are the existential
coordinates that need to balance the former. These existential
aspects emphasize the temporality of the educative, the conjoining of life histories which creates the possibility of mutuality. Just as his letter to A calls for an equilibrium, a balance
of forces, the positional and situational aspects of educational
roles must also find their equilibrium.

How then does this distinction between a sequence of

stages (positional consciousness) and a concurrence of dimensions (situational consciousness) clarify educative events? As
B made clear to us, the helper exercises his need to help by
practicing his own disunity in relationship to the struggles to
become of another. His own struggle limits what he will be
able to apprehend. But what he reveals in his act opens the
possibility of mutuality. The basic assumption upon which
the educator takes his stand is this relationship between positional and situational consciousnesses. If the educator is
minded to view life development as a sequence of stages
(positional), so that his task is only to raise up to his level one
who is lower down, then there is a fundamental disequilibrium which will prevent the development of both the educator and the one to be educated. The more opaque the educator's need to be another's helper, the more hidden is the basis
and source from which new life is to come. The edifice of
knowledge often hides the real source of light and development. Similarly, if the one to be educated holds the view that
he is the lower, then the passivity of his attitude perpetuates
illusion of growth. The respect and appreciation for human
development grows out of the work of self-knowledge, which
is the experience of being constantly at a limit and of striving
to unify the paradoxical characters that we are. The recognition of limit and the process of making it transparent to the
other is crucial to the true life of service. There will always be
a misunderstanding between the helper and the helped unless
they establish a fundamental "equality" in their relationship.
The idea of stages can function both positively and negatively in relationship to this experience of equality. For if the
helper presents himself as one who is more advanced along
the way in a distinct series of stages, he will be likely to
offend the individual to be helped, in the sense of undermining his freedom to develop his own uniqueness, and of
letting himself come to represent the truth of experience as if
possessing it rather than standing beside or in the light of
truth. The helped individual will see his task as either to emu-
late a rule or to try to steal away the possessions of the helper,

seductively or by direct assault. When the notion of stages of development is used to portray the positions of a lower and a higher status between individuals, and when there is not a corresponding situational understanding, then the helper has alienated himself or has become alienated from the person to be helped. When this is the case, neither individual will be able to develop in relation to the other since the relationship is built upon false premises, which themselves will have to be destroyed if there is to be learning. From this it is perhaps clear why there is the kind of educational violence in our time and why development is couched in such violent terms and acts. When the potential helper stands in the way of that which could enable the other to be helped, he must be denied, overthrown, ridiculed, ignored, or made aware of his own needs. The attack on positional consciousness is often engaged through efforts to despatialize. These may be expressed by satire, irony, and comedy—forms which draw attention to the situational as a shift from spatial to temporal conditions.

The orientation toward the idea of life stages can function as a means to self-knowledge. It serves as a tool of penetration which clarifies the helper's role and his understanding of the nature of the goals of educating. When the helper also learns to celebrate the situation of his own inner struggles with the other who is in need, then need and neededness will be joined in creative communion. As the many-sided event shows us, each person is engaged in his respective appropriation process. That they are different, that one knows more than the other, that one is more experienced and better able to help in some specific way, these factors are not doubted. But these factors need the animation and creative potential which only come about through a mutual experience of equality.

A discussion of the educator and of a word like equality suggests that we are in danger of gravitating toward an event based primarily upon moral sentiment and democratic idealism, both of which forms of thought are inadequate as a ground for the kind of practice that our age, and indications of future challenges, present to us. Equality implies justice, that the law protects and preserves a likeness of power. Equality then, from the foregoing, would mean something like "evenness of stature," occupying equivalent positions in life. The image for equality is spatial. But let us look once more at our allegory. B's invitation to A is that, through giving birth to himself, A will become a friend to B. Friendship, for B, means "the sharing of perspective." The perspective he strives to open is the depth of an experience that is essentially historical: a presence to self. The shared perspective is a temporal one, for the quality of the experience of time is a way of seeing that bestows value and meaning upon a world. We also saw that another story stood behind B's invitation and invocation: by making a friend, Judge William could resolve a paradox of self-integration, placing himself fully within the domain of the universal-human, the completeness of being. This enterprise was left incomplete, but it affects the meaning of the word equality in the present discussion.

Equality means, then, evenness, a like potential for freedom. Our special attention to the word reveals that equality furthermore means a shared ground, a recognized commonness, and most importantly, a shared sense of belonging to a common temporal dimension, the historical meeting that we call the many-sided event.

There is a conception of justice in every act of help. To the idea of equal stature our allegorical reading brings us the recognition of a common temporality. A shared stage of life puts us on the same level, coexistence; but a shared historical dimension evokes a world that, by enabling us to release our creative abilities, forms a community of contemporaries.

When one generation educates another, the consequences of motivation in the older confront the formation of motivation in the younger. The goals of education must include the experience of contemporaneity between two generations, their being present for one another. There are two dimensions in the educational situation: one, the explicit, spatial educational setting and procedure (e.g., the classroom); the other, the implicit engagement between personal histories of teachers and pupils. Two educative experiences correspond to these two time dimensions: one, the content of the educational process; and two, the way in which this content is expressed and the impression it makes upon the pupil. The example of a study made on teacher motivation may help to illustrate our exploration of the second temporal dimension of interacting personal histories, and subsequently of the idea of human becoming.

An analysis of anecdotes written by teachers describing important experiences in family life and schooling revealed the extent to which the teacher was engaged in unfinished business, reworking a particular experience, revisiting the scene of a difficulty or success, or, in general, trying to complete a historical event by recreating the situation anew.[3] The study disclosed the fact that for a large percentage of individuals, the choice of a teaching career and of the particular age and grade of the pupils they desired to teach, coincided with a strong personal experience in a similar situation during the teacher's own development. In some cases the anecdote, which appeared to be saying that a teacher's experience with a negative identity figure had repelled them in an opposite direction to such a negative influence, in fact revealed upon closer analysis of that individual that a negative reaction could result in a similarly negative expression of feeling, though the content of the action might appear to be different. To impose the negative or positive lesson of a historical event is nevertheless to impose upon another person or a group. What is experienced is the act of imposing. The consequences in the classroom will often be the unexpected and confusing reaction of the pupils toward whom the teacher intended to be positively disposed. The paradigm of identification and the exercising of personal history are crucial factors of career motivation and professional style. The degree of achievement, effectiveness, and personal fulfillment are especially influenced by these historical factors.[4]

The example of teacher motivation cited above is meant to

indicate the resources and limits an individual brings to bear in a situation of help. The effort to complete unfinished chapters of an autobiography is the hidden appropriation process that usually remains unrecognized. Its richness is rarely shared except inadvertently as the consequence of influences experienced by others (pupils, colleagues) through subtle communications eluding the awareness that could have evoked more satisfactory responses.

The concealed motives of personal history participate decisively in the daily encounters of those who stand in the posture of helpers, who are entrusted with the roles of aiding and improving the growth processes of others. The skepticism of our age, which is turned against the authority of service institutions, is confirmed by this analysis if, as is often assumed, the personal motives of members of service professions function mainly to contradict and restrict their usefulness: where position and situation stand in contradictory relationship. This skepticism, beside its political and ideological implications, introduces a lack of credibility reflecting an uncertainty about any person's competency to assume the posture of helper or for people to have confidence in the ability of others to minister to their needs. To lack this initial trust is to decide not to share our futures, and hence to fail to become contemporaries.

Motive is not only a conditioned structure of the past, it is also a principle of future development. The implications of undertaking an analysis of teacher motivation are that a greater awareness of interacting historical conflicts will liberate some of the energy that is invested in silencing before others the stories that we tell ourselves about our work—histories, though unacknowledged, which become interdependent and which hold the promise of a true educative communality.

The exclusiveness of stages is broken when we discover that to exist means not only to hold a position, to be a spatial particularity, but to experience oneself in a history whose present includes memory and anticipation, signifying a participation in a wholeness of time which is our situation of simultaneity. We are called upon to affirm the participation in a wholeness of being with the wholeness of another. If, in the relationship of helper to helped, this event appears one-sided, where one party only receives and the other only gives, and a mutuality is denied, then place and particularity are asserted as predominant. The event establishes an essential inequality and a hierarchy that alienates not only person from person, but inner aspects of a single individual. The project of the future remains a "private" endeavor, a denial of the interdependence of human development.

This ultimately unsuccessful conception of existing as spatial exclusiveness is broken by B when he announces that not the particular stage of life but rather the movement is primary for understanding development. He introduces the quality of existence which transforms a sequence of stages into the affirmed dimensions of an event.

An eventful education occurs primarily through language. We should not be too surprised to discover that the idea of human dispositions exhibited in the variety of *Either/Or*'s linguistic embodiments becomes, for Kierkegaard's later work, the prefiguration of varieties of human discourse. What we have been speaking about as an event formed through juxtaposition of relationships becomes the occasion of communication between speakers and listeners, yielding the consequences for education of forms of communication.

PART III

Enabling Communication

Preface

The psychology of personality and development, with its concern for the stages of development, is paralleled in each one of us who regards his and her life as a journey and who would seek to know how the configuration of events discloses the distinct chapters of an autobiography. In our reading of *Either/Or* we became acquainted with characters belonging to qualitatively different life dispositions. We found these dispositions to be metaphorically categorized variously as attitudes, stages, and spheres of human becoming. We explored the implications of these terms as they help to identify the spatio-temporal dimension of human development, paying special attention to the shift from understanding human becoming in positional terms, with emphasis on role, goal, and placement of an individual in a hierarchical ordering of stages, to understanding the situational character of human becoming, in which mutuality, process, and simultaneity of dimensions of self are discovered. The movement from positional to situational consciousness involves despatializing the former conception and attending existentially to the temporality or interior historical reality of the individual. Positional and situational consciousness are complementary; nevertheless, one often finds a conflict of views with regard to which orientation should predominate in a given instance

—education being a particularly critical area. The existential contribution to such problems consists in its exploration of human becoming as the concrete historical reality of the individual from whose situation it attempts to build. The outcome of this is its correcting the balance between goal and process life orientations, which reminds us that however much our lives seem to have direction and motivation, the energy animating human becoming has its origin in the multidimensional interpretation of concurrent aspects of self. The fully human presence to one another of such individuals, given this understanding, is the groundwork for a true meeting of contemporaries. That historical intersection reveals the potential for what we have come to call the educative event.

Kierkegaard as educative thinker is the author of the educative event we explored in *Either/Or*. A fuller, more conceptual and detailed account of life dispositions is contained in several subsequent works of Kierkegaard's pseudonymous authorship. Of these, the most concise is found in his major philosophical work, *Concluding Unscientific Postscript* (1846). There he persists in using the term "stages" (*Stadier*) in conceptualizing human becoming. As we shall see, life stages represent particular value perspectives organized according to a person's relationship to their experience of temporality. But we shall also discover that these modes of "existence interpretations" (*existents-opfattelser*) can also be grasped as "existence communications" (*existents-meddelelser*). The transition from the concept to the communication of existence will bring us back to the heart of educative events such as we first introduced with the characters of *Either/Or*. Educative events become now acts of speech aimed at promoting the fullest attainment of human possibility. The limits of such possibilities and the language meant to serve them bring us to consider the relationship between education and communication. Such a momentous exploration ought to be introduced by a rather lighter task of preparation.

Consider the communication of motive in the following little tale featuring another sort of educator, one whom Kierkegaard wrote about in his *Journal* for 1847.

A corporal of the militia says to a newly recruited farm-hand: "Now then, you are to hold yourself erect." Recruit: "Yes, I will do that." Corporal: "Yes, and then you are not to speak while shouldering arms." Recruit: "Oh, mustn't I? Well then just as you say, Sir." Corporal: "The devil! I said that you are not to speak while shouldering arms." Recruit: "Yes, yes, don't be angry. Now I know that I must not speak. I'll remember to keep quiet while bearing arms, Sir."[1]

What? we exclaim. Is the corporal also supposed to be an educator? Yes, for although we do not know the corporal's personal motives, his stance in this farcical story is to enable the new recruit to learn how to be a good soldier. The corporal is administrating the law by giving commands intended to help the recruit become part of the rule rather than an exception. The corporal is in this sense an educator, though of the old school—which has nevertheless managed to survive quite well. Something unexpected, however, happens here; something which makes the tale comical. If we weigh the corporal's assertive commands against the recruit's passive understanding, which causes him to do the opposite of the command while at the same time acknowledging it, then we encounter a contradiction, a misunderstanding. If we saw the event acted out in the style of an old-time slapstick routine, much of the comical effect would come from gestures and facial expressions. We gain a certain amount of pleasure from seeing the figure of authority, the corporal, stymied by the paradoxical responses of the recruit. It is the good-naturedness of the recruit which makes the little act even more pleasant, since there is further ambiguity in his responses, leaving us to wonder whether he is a fool or a clever trickster. Kierkegaard gives the theme of this brief drama in a note just preceding it, which reads: "An example of the misunderstanding that conceives an education in competency as an education in knowledge."

The tale of the corporal and the recruit illustrates the discrepancy between "knowing about" and "being able." Kierkegaard uses it in several different drafts of a lecture concerned with the dialectics of communication (*meddelelsens dialektik*).[2] It figures as a kind of fable for a series of lectures, which he never gave, concerned with what he called *kunnens dialektik*, which we translate as "the dialectic of competency." Taking both dialectical terms together, and focusing upon the role of the one who shares (*dele*) his abilities with (*med*) another, the informant (*meddeler*), we may understand Kierkegaard's art as an "enabling dialectic." The fable, then, announces the transition we have been exploring: from the conception of stages, to that of the intersection of temporal dimensions—the shared moment or event, which now becomes the "dialectic of discourse." Let us proceed slowly through this transition.

The recruit knows about or understands the objective intent of the corporal's command; he merely fails to appropriate the information into his proficiency as a soldier bearing arms. He knows what he should do, and at some point he will do it, but thus far the communications has missed its mark in shaping the immediate behavior of the recruit. Possibly the recruit will always only *know about* what he is supposed to do, and in knowing about it will fail to make the next step, transforming the communication into an action. The communication tells the recruit what to do, it advises him under command, but it does not say how the recruit is to receive this communication. He should respond obediently to a command issued from within a closed context of meaning which operates upon the assumption that the Good is that which derives from the chain of command or hierarchy. But his failure to recognize this primary assumption of authority places him outside its effectiveness, at least in this fictive account. Ultimately, the communication is rendered absurd should we consider the whole episode. If the message is meaningless in terms of effectiveness, the corporal (informant) if also rendered ineffective: he becomes angry because his position is inauthenticated.

The corporal has simply assumed that to command the knowledge of what a good recruit should do is identical with the recruit's appropriation of the message. But knowing about and being able, capable, or competent in relationship to a command is not the same thing. The object of knowledge is cast into an ambiguous status. The sufficiency of the informant's posture (his rank) is also made dubious. And the recipient's (the recruit's) situation at the other end of the command is also put into suspension. We are on the way toward recasting the story of A and B.

Kierkegaard lets this little fable of a misunderstanding be an illustration of the situation in which the communication of an object of knowledge fails to result in the expected behavior of the recipient. The situation is appropriate because the context is military, the institution responsible for the protection of nation and value, perhaps analogous to the defenders of culture. The story of the corporal and the recruit is allegorical or becomes so in the context that concerns the situation of individuals in the realm of the ethical, the common good. The story serves to draw our attention to other situations in which a communication is initially aimed at improving or edifying, toward orientating in the sphere of the moral good. The status of objective knowledge between the informant and the recipient, and of the nature of the communication's assumption, reintroduces us to the educator's dilemma. In the humanistic sphere, where to educate is always ultimately directed at orientation toward a conception of the good, the just, and the morally right, the situation of the educator is dependent upon his understanding of what it is to disclose an object of knowledge such that the appropriation of that knowledge completes the circle of meaning. Or, putting it a little differently, the teacher who uses language, who depends upon speaking and writing, needs an awareness of the art of discourse which is not merely programmatic or sophistical, but which reflects the mode of appropriation from the side of the informant. The metacommunication is, then, that the recipient gains the understanding that to know what is communicated is also to realize the nature of the communication.

The kind of communication which the helper undertakes Kierkegaard calls "indirect communication" (*indirekte med-*

delelse). This should not be understood as simply a device of language or a form of rhetoric, for then we arrive once again at a situation of inequality and misunderstanding. Indirect communication evokes the temporal dimension because in it is reflected the speaker's own ongoing life process and possibility rather than a final result, which shows no development. There are various modes of indirect communication, as we shall see. Some of them may seem even more direct or intimate than what are supposedly encounters of immediate access. What is indirect is the reflected mode of the speaker's appropriation process, his orientation in the realm of the object where he makes himself the object of consciousness, reflecting himself in his task of living through an experience whose finality is always ahead of him as a project directed toward a future. The appropriateness of the communication grows out of the mode of appropriation, for which the informant (the speaker, author) bears responsibility. There is an autobiographical presence that reveals itself in the *how* as well as in the *what* of communication. It is this factor that attracts us to the autobiographical, in which the *how* of a person's life is disclosed as an invitation to human possibility.

It is the temporal status of the individuals which makes for the dialectic of indirect communication, since they must first direct themselves to their own individual futures if they are to discover one another. They discover one another when they see, by means of action, that they share a common future, that they share in a common development of a possible fulfillment: they partake in the historical because they take part in their own individual historical consciousnesses.

Indirect communication aims to bring forth the realization that for both the informant and the would-be recipient, there is a task that remains to be fulfilled. Direct communication, a mode of discourse usually assumed in the sciences, in which the object of knowledge is the objective of inquiry, can also have a future orientation, which is the solution of anomalies, the construction of new paradigms, in short, "advancement." It is assumed in the domain of scientific communication that the object has a more or less independent status. The project of scientific knowledge, which also has its helping aspects, appears to be terminable upon the adequate relationship of the concept with the object under observation. The truth of knowledge in the scientific domain is the isomorphic relationship that obtains between description, explanation, law, and the data of observation which reconfirms the consistency of the law.

The process invoked by indirect communication requires a qualitative change on the side of the recipient, i.e., that the recipient experience a qualitative change in apprehending himself as the knower. The objective status disappears or is transformed by the experience of development on the part of the knower, i.e., into self-knowledge. The result, if it can be called that, is indirect communication's "consequentiality" rather than simply its termination. There are always further consequences to every act of participation in the sphere of humanistic knowledge, where the ethical is raised into view. The communication must be faithful to the interminability of its undertaking, and must be clear—or as Kierkegaard says, "transparent"—about its consequences. The educator learns through the event of speaking and discourse the nature of consequence for both sides. His task is to keep the discourse open, to let himself be known in it, to know himself in his communication, and to take care within the limits of language for himself and for the other, for the learner, the recipient.

9.

Eventful Discourse

All discussions of life disposition in Kierkegaard's authorship fall *inside* the framework of his indirect discourse. Is it possible then that Kierkegaard's life-stages idea is meant to do more than enable us to place a structure over our actions and the behavior of others? Is he in some way evoking and confronting *how* we interpret outselves? As we examine the role of life stages we shall discover ourselves turning toward the *gestalt* of personal history. Personal history is a way of viewing and apprehending ourselves and others. Through it we make actions significant and give them the status of events to be interpreted. The expressive quality of experience is specifically studied in language and these moments of documented stages are seen to become kinds of "eventful discourses."

Let us begin by taking two instances where the stages are summarized. The first is found in a subsection of the *Postscript* entitled, "The Decisive Expression." The summary occurs as a footnote to a paragraph dealing with the consciousness of guilt. Guilt consciousness is characteristic of the ethical man's realization that as a finite "exister" responsible within a historical awareness (his finite freedom) he is nevertheless remote from the perfection and highest station of virtue, which, in this case, is signified by an "eternal happiness." The discovery of a seemingly unbreachable separation from the eternal produces a qualitative change in the individual, an intensified realization that for every leap forward there is a corresponding fall downward. The individual—whom we might associate with B in his sketch of himself as an exception to the universal human—stands incompatibly related or in disrelationship to the highest, the eternal.[1] The footnote appears appended to this word, "disrelationship," thus implying that the stages are constructs emerging from incongruities between the finite (historical point of departure) and the infinite (eternal happiness). Instead of the three spheres depicted in *Either/Or* there are now apparently seven rungs on a ladder of ascent.

> Immediacy; finite common sense; irony; ethics with irony as incognito; humor, religiousness with humor as incognito; and then finally the Christian religiousness, recognizable by the paradoxical accentuation of existence, by the paradox, by the breach with immanence, and by the absurd.[2]

The origin and termination of stages, immediacy/absurdity, are puzzling landmarks for a journey of self. Are we to understand the life process as lying between pure undifferentiated being (immediacy) and completely paradoxically-differentiated existence (the absurd): There is more here in the way of movement than of rest. Our first clue arises when we notice that these stages display an oscillation between the poles of limit and unlimit. Immediacy is pure unlimitedness, finite common sense is limitedness, irony is again unlimit (a limitlessness defined in *Concept of Irony* as "infinite absolute negativity"), ethics portrayed through the mask of irony is limitedness disguised by limitlessness (the Socratic), humor swings toward limitlessness (infinite resignation, the laugh that resolves all conflict), the religious under the appearance of humor portrays a paradoxical limit situation indicating perhaps that the two poles are nearing together, approaching a unity, or rather a collision. We take note that the rhythm and movement of this dialectic—limit/limitless—refers essentially to temporal determinations of being. Let us consider the second summary in the *Postscript*.

The second recapitulation stands under Section B, "The Dialectical" (Section A was called "Existential Pathos," of which "The Decisive Expression" was subsection three). The task in this instance concerns the various "interpretations of existence" which are ranked in accordance with the degree of an "individual's apprehension of inwardness."[3] First comes a warning: speculative philosophy (a mode of interpretation) has no authentic role to play in relationship to the stages. The warning continues by declaring that speculative philosophy (i.e., metaphysics, and most essentially Hegelianism) deals with a concept of "mankind," which is its pure idea, whereas what is about to follow concerns neither mankind as a whole nor the relative differences between men. For whom then are these stages meant? we ask. For "thyself," is echoed back. But who is thyself? This unspoken question adds an extradimensional framework of reference serving the reader as an instrument of reflection. It is the question that Socrates carried from Delphi to the *agora* and one that Kierkegaard revived in his own market town. Revealing the stages as an allegory of the self, Kierkegaard intimates them as a Jacob's ladder. The pseudonymous author of the *Postscript* bears the name of Johannes Climacus, author of the fifth century manuscript, *The Ladder of Divine Ascent*. He proceeds to list four stages of interpretation: the aesthetic, ethical, religiousness A, and the paradoxical religiousness.[4] We may assume for the moment that the first three stages are roughly equivalent to those discussed in the context of *Either/Or*. We follow the refraction of meaning created by bringing the stages together with a second frame of reference which helps to evoke the sense of allegory—indirect communication.

The title page of the section on dialectics says quite simply, "Time." The summary of stages under this heading is repeated twice, first as "existence-interpretation" and second as "existence-communication." Interpretation and communication become the two media that reflect the meaning of stages. They are complementary in suggesting a process like breathing: taking in and letting out, impression and expression. The existence-interpretation echoes the first stages which tell or outline "what it is to exist." The communication of existence tells "how it is to be existing."

Kierkegaard offers us a "comment" this time instead of a footnote. He suggests how the dialectical stages could be understood. We are to recall the previous short work, *Philosophical Fragments* (1844), to which this lengthy work serves as a postscript. The *Fragments* deals with topics like learning and teaching, Socrates and Christ as teachers, with the finite and infinite human project—historical and eternal happiness. If the stages are then applied retrospectively we arrive at the following illustrations. First, the aesthetical view: there is a master and a pupil, the pupil becomes a master and he acquires *his* pupil, and so on. Truth, like the relationship between master and pupil, is relative, first the one and then the other has it. But second, viewed from the religious perspective, there is neither teacher nor pupil, except insofar as the teacher is an "occasion" for the pupil's discovery of himself and the limitlessness of self-knowledge, his eternal validity. Every individual is equally related to and equidistant from the eternal. The third illustration is the one for the paradoxical-religiousness: the Deity is the teacher; he, the eternal one, enters time (hence the paradox of the finite and the infinite) and creates not only a new self-knowledge but gives as well the condition for a new creature, a rebirth. The first religious view, entitled A, is affirmed as the highest authentic mode of assistance between man and man. The second, labeled B, is later revealed as Christianity, and is a relationship holding between man and God.[5]

Instead of seven stages we find four. Instead of four illustrations we find only three. If Kierkegaard meant the stages model as a direct application of structures he would certainly not have left us with ambiguous and inconsistent depictions of development. We are led to wonder where the author is in relationship to his life stages, just as we know that when our own moments of development become explicit to us we are actually beyond our self-consciousness and entering new unknown territories.

Viewed in another way, the stages can be seen to serve several different purposes. The seven-stage model illustrates movement and transition, the dialectic of disrelationship and incongruity. The four-stage model focuses upon spheres or domains which are, by virtue of their respective consequences, mutually exclusive life attitudes. The first model indicates the appropriation of a world of value and meaning; the second, the expression or communication of how it is to be so oriented. The seven-stage model not only gives us an impression of movement between stages, but of the inner and outer faces of being, which are more appropriately called "spheres" because they have interfacings—incommensurabilities between the internal and external, as we saw in *Either/Or*.

Seven, four, and three: is Kierkegaard playing with sacred numbers: Is he turning the stages of development into a personal myth? The myth of stages of life serves something like Plato's "Divided Line" (see *Republic*, book six) or the "seven mansions" in St. Theresa's *Interior Castle*. The stages are allegorical and they point to a central problem: unity. We recall what Kierkegaard has said in his *Journals*: "it is not the path which is the problem, rather the problem *is* the path." It is the way toward a unity.

A study of Kierkegaard's discussion of stages in his earlier *Journals* reveals that he takes as his primary basis the idea of unity that Augustine evokes through his examination of the meaning of the Trinity, that three is also One.[6] For Augustine it is the mysterious wholeness of three mutually exclusive qualities: of time, for example, where the wholeness of time is composed of memory, of understanding, and will or faith: the past, present, and future orientations of being. For Kierkegaard, as with Augustine, there is not static synthesis but convergence, a movement toward fulfillment or what Kierkegaard called "the fullness of time."

Kierkegaard illustrates the stages by three eventful meetings: a relative one of higher and lower; an equal one between Socrates and his pupil (where the ethical and religious
are combined in the Socratic posture); and one that is neither
relative nor equal but an absolutely paradoxical meeting between an individual and the Divine—the revelatory experience. Recall that the dialectic of these eventful meetings rests
under the heading "time." Augustine's trinity of time is implicated in the illustration from *Philosophical Fragments.* Socrates is made to stand for the Greek doctrine of *anamnesis,*
recollection. His use of the doctrine is later (and earlier, in
Concept of Irony) explained as an irony that helps to create
the occasion of self-remembrance—presence to self, the present. Christ and the paradoxical nature of the Christian story
points toward the future, hope, and the newness of being.
We are directed to consider the meaning of temporality in
relationship to these eventful meetings and their mode of discourse. We are invited and encouraged to take up the reflected part of communication about stages, that they are
temporal modes of discourse; they are events the description
of which is also an event.

We question, however, whether these stages are meant as
explanatory structures of reality. Is Kierkegaard not provid-
ing us with a system by which we locate ourselves and try to
predict our destiny—an "existential system"? No more than
Augustine resolves the mystery of a temporal unity does
Kierkegaard provide a resolved paradigm. We are forewarned early in the *Postscript* that an existential system is an
impossibility.[7] Only God could comprehend such an order of
actuality because such a formulation as the unity of actuality
is equivalent to the finality of existence. In order to think
existence through, thought must overcome the temporality of
its own process and emerge as the perfect and timeless crystal
of being. What kind of thinking process could transcend the
finitude of its own advance, could derive its own immortality
by assessing the situation of its mortality? There has always
been this effort in metaphysics, to bring time to a halt, to
dwell in a realm of essences free from the gravitational pull of

the earth's temporality. Thinking is a process animated by the will and powered by the batteries of memory. By thinking in terms of stages can an individual climb the rungs of the ladder of ascent, determine his own destiny and control his future? Thinking that is controlling makes identity its motive. Thought wills to be the same as that which makes thought possible. When thought is able to think itself, as Hegel puts it, then there is an identity of the finite process with the infinite structure; time would be abrogated and existence comprehended as a whole, a rational totality. The idea of stages is tempting: it seems that one could get a foothold in the world and then simply climb up the ladder into the eternal kingdom. But Kierkegaard suggests that there is another kind of thinking then controlling and willing cognition. There is another motive than identity between being and thinking. The project of thought which seeks to identify itself with the power that makes thought itself possible is able to do so by abstracting itself from its own conditions, i.e., from existence. Of course there is great beauty and an ecstacy in this accomplishment whenever it is possible. But the reapplication of thought that has freed itself from all temporal processes returning to stand victoriously over existence is like the man who is master of his own development—he is always at an end looking back. The only requirement for such an accomplishment is the denial of life itself. But this is not the way of Kierkegaard's Christianity.

The underlying current in Kierkegaard's description of the life stages gives us a sense for the projected wholeness of being and for the unity we seek, which is not the effort to become identical with that which makes our life possible, but to belong, as fully as possible, to the process of becoming. The quest for identity, when made the ultimate motive of self-development, strives to bring time to a halt. The motive of possession and control of developmental forces may serve to increase a sense of self, but that self is fictive, since it is always at its own life termination before there is a true beginning. The curious effect of Kierkegaard's discourse on the stages is to produce an opposite result from that which one might at first think. We are encouraged to give up the quest for possession of self-identity and the conquering of the powers of life development. We are encouraged to belong to a process of thought which strives to release itself toward a fulfillment by increasing its participation in the life process. We discover ourselves when we give ourselves up to the unknown toward which we are drawn. The stages help us to celebrate the not knowing who we are. But they also help us to remember that this unknown, the futurity of being, calls to each of us in a different voice. Only each single one can discern that voice and respond. And it is to that voice that we wish to bear witness.

Our discussion of Kierkegaard's stages as part of an indirect discourse yields three aspects of development: movement, interpretation, and communication or expression. When emphasis is placed upon existence—the actuality that our motives are trying to bring about—because time is required to think the matter through and to describe it, then we acknowledge that such an expression of existence will have to be consistent with its discovery and not give the appearance of finality which is implied by a system. A system implies an independent harmony of interrelated ideas, principles, rules, procedures, and laws. What Kierkegaard calls for is discourse that reveals the individual situated in the event of his speaking, that communicates the passing of time and the aging of the speaker. The communication that takes place along with the "absence of a system" is one of the ways in which Kierkegaard explains indirect communication.[8] Indirect communication further implies a faithfulness to the moment in which one speaks, a trueness consistent with a thought process seeking to release itself into a deeper participation with life and therefore with others, a process that continues to think expressively by revealing the subject in his development. Expressive thinking about self-development means that in revealing ourselves we throw light on others whom we have invited to participate with us. The ecstacy we experience in discovering ourselves is sharable since we have uncovered the hidden processes impelling the strivings of others in their quest for wholeness. In sharing we express our gratitude: appropriation and devotion become unified in our personal histories.

The witness does not aim to persuade or to explain, his task is to testify to the truth of his own development.[9] Like Socrates in the *Gorgias* (472c) speaking to Polus, the "witness" testifies in order to produce a "single witness" in the other. The difference between dialogue and rhetoric is just this witnessing: each participant becomes able to carry through his own attestations to their fullest consequences. Socrates aims to evoke the witness in the other, the opponent, encouraging him to join in the process of clarifying the issue at hand. He knows that they will not reach each other unless a clearing is made enabling both to become fully present to each other. Witnessing opens up the possibility of confirmation and mutuality. By thinking about stages of life can we learn to become witnesses for one another?

With this question we enter upon a central problem in the discussion of the stages. The stages testify to a process whereby an individual undertakes a journey toward actuality. But how do individuals come to play a role in each other's journeys? The Socrates we have been discussing seems primarily concerned about his self-actuality rather than that of others, about his knowing only himself as an actuality.[10] Perhaps by thinking about stages of life we become more self-transparent but just as opaque to one another in terms of our experience of the moral perfection to which we minister. The problem with the stages is that though they make reference to events of mutuality they seem not to contain any account of intersubjectivity—how we participate in each other's actuality. Perhaps we can only witness and affirm ourselves.

It is generally true that the scope of Kierkegaard's philosophical writing does not include a theory of mutuality and participation between individuals in the self-actualization process. Nor do we find such a theory with Socrates. Nevertheless the Greek and the Dane managed to instill their thoughts in the minds and hearts of others, participating their actuality in the developmental process of later generations. It is difficult to say whether theirs was a strength or a weakness, with regard to such a theory. What would proof of intersubjectivity have amounted to? Does not Socratic dialogue and Kierkegaardian dialectics testify to a common ground? Perhaps this is why Kierkegaard's stages (like Socratic ignorance) remain unfinished: they are ingredients for thought rather than prepackaged dinners. We cannot overlook the world that a thinker's style opens to us. We repeat, with Kierkegaard, that the *how* of a speaker's discourse becomes or shapes the *what*, the thought content. The *how* is the test and testimony of the *what*. This does not mean, however, that the means of communication is the message communicated; rather, the thinker's style is the voice of the witness which informs the authenticity of the communication's contents.

If we examine the nature of Kierkegaard's indirect communication, we find so far that there are three modes: character portrayal and pseudonym, communication of process rather than of system (result), and witnessing. The common denominator of these is the existential quality that Kierkegaard terms the "communication of possibility." We have seen in repeated cases that even with the intimacy of the witness there remains a fundamental separation. This separation can then be understood in two ways: first, as the struggle for self-integration; and, second, as the desire and need for mutual assistance signified by the reunion of individuals, for example, A and B. What Kierkegaard implies, and that to which his writing testifies, is the service we perform for one another in completing the unfinished chapters of our autobiographies. He does not allow this process to become sentimentalized, where the significance of values outleaps the structure of possibility. In pursuing certain Kierkegaardian, though also universal themes it is easy enough to become either a sentimental enthusiast or a "virtuous" critic. Either way assumes that Kierkegaard's problem is not our problem. We could also try to share the difficulty that he makes available. That is the alternative we are trying to celebrate here.

The underlying problem of the stage is, as has been stated, one of unity, the overcoming of certain basic incommensurabilities in the process of becoming whole. Curiously, without these incongruities of being, we would never embark upon such a journey. The dynamic principle of unity leads us to recognize a second problem, self-transcendence. Accordingly, we have identified two kinds of transcendencies in the ethical realm (between man and man): first, the ability of the human spirit to journey from a set of limiting conditions to a set of possibilities, which are then made actual; and, second, the right and responsibility of individuals to be of service to one another, being-for-another. These two aspects of transcendence involve human justice. We invite and involve others in our processes of becoming whole. But there is a third kind of transcendence which is only possible through Divine intervention, and this is grace.

Clearly, when Kierkegaard speaks of "eternal" and of an individual's authentic relationship to it, he assumes something about God's love for humanity. He assumes the power that bestows a gift of new life. It does not lie within the range of human powers to make such a gift, nor is it appropriate between man and man to pretend to such power. But within the human dimension of transcendence this power is reflected and made possible, it is the care we extend to one another. This act of care is related to our conception of the eternal. Kierkegaard reconstructs the entire problematic of stages in terms of a caring dialectic, an enabling mode of discourse which seeks to be faithful to its conception and apprehension of that which is unspeakable, the eternal.

Kierkegaard presents another formulation of the stages as existence-communications in the notes he was preparing for the series of lectures on the "dialectics of competency" (*Kunnens Meddelser*), or, as understood within the context of indirect communication, the art that demonstrates an "enabling dialectic." There are three striking features of this dialectic's discourse which further our inquiry of the stages seen as events. First, there are, once again, the three types of communication: aesthetic, ethical, and religious. Second, communication is described not simply as the position of a speaker but as a *situation* whose meaning involves an informant and a recipient, a content, and a reflection of that content. The communication is to be understood as a whole made up of the participation from both sides contributing to and reflecting a set of consequences. The intent of this formulation at first appears to be concerned with the informant's awareness of how he situates himself in relationship to the recipient and in relationship to the event that his communication creates. But the situation could just as easily be concerned with how the recipient situates himself as listener or reader. Third, the stages as modes of discourse fall under the general category of reflected communication, they are modes of discourse which disclose "how" participants are involved with "what" they communicate.[11]

The easiest form of dialectics to understand of the three is the second, the ethical. It is modeled upon the Socratic figure who turns a dialogue from the simple persuasion of views to the consideration of what it means to hold those views, i.e., the focus or reflection is upon the subject. The Socratic goal is to reveal to the opponent the consequences of his opinions for himself, to let the other discover self-contradiction: not why he is in error but how—an ignorance that calls upon the individual to reflect upon his situation, making him open (or at least vulnerable) to the possibility of true knowledge.

The effect of discourse which orients the recipient toward an awareness of his present attitudes and prepares him receptively for an appropriation process is the ethical "art" of discourse. The art is the enabling that directs itself toward an educative goal (*paeideia*) rather than toward a persuasive one (rhetoric). The effect of the ethical mode is to enjoin the other to participate reflectively in a project aimed at the Good, i.e., the universal aim of all actualizing process. This discovery of the Good and of its principles was discussed in *Philosophical Fragments* within the general framework of an individual's quest for happiness. This quest for happiness was simply assumed, as was the fact that men seek for an abiding happiness in some eternal reality. The teacher, Socrates, serves as "occasion" for the pupil's discovery of his eternality. This discovery was characterized as an "instant" of self-transcendence, Socrates and the learner both vanishing into the infinity of the timelessness of truth. But this timelessness of truth was further characterized as a pagan conception of the eternal: a nontemporal preexistent state of the soul which can be regained through a process of recollection (*anamnesis*). The Christian transcendence was contradistinguished to this and hence does not fall within the ethical communication.

The first form of discourse, the aesthetical, is puzzling. Kierkegaard says that under this mode the reflection of communication falls equally upon informant and recipient, whereas with the ethical form the reflection is directed primarily toward the recipient. In the aesthetical mode they are joined to a common object through the production of a feeling. Informant, recipient, and object all participate in the immediacy of the beautiful. The aesthetical communication, though reflected, serves to unite participants in a moment of feeling with the object—the poem, painting, song. Curiously, Kierkegaard considers even his *Either/Or* under the category of the aesthetical, not because it concerns only aesthetic topics (which of course it does not) but because the mode of communication aims primarily to provoke a *feeling for* the situation of the three speakers, i.e., possibility. Perhaps Kierkegaard could foresee that *Either/Or* would be read mainly for pleasure or for the sake of the "interesting."

The third mode of discourse, the religious, like the ethical, directs reflection toward the recipient's own process of development and decision. But this time the teacher bears "new knowledge" and is the condition for the learner's "new life." The teacher who is the condition of rebirth is Christ, and hence we have the Christian transcendence. Those who serve devotedly the religious mode of communication reflect their relationship to this new life by preparing the recipient for the transforming words of Scripture. But, for Kierkegaard, this preparation does not mean using the authority of the Church to show the Divine command behind the ethical "ought," it means revealing oneself as a witness to the truth of transformation or rebirth.

The structure of the dialectical discourse which facilitates through indirect communication gives a new possibility to the understanding of stages or spheres of life orientation. They are consequential modes of communication. Each reflects how the participants are related to the object of the discourse by assuming that this relationship determines the quality of that in which they participate. Let us go no further without saying that clearly for Kierkegaard the religious discourse is the most consequential or the discourse with the fullest potential while posing the greatest difficulty. He insists that throughout his authorship the religious orientation was the ultimate concern of his dialectical discourse; it was the deepest dimension, because the one most intensifying the factors of pathos and paradox by holding the finite and infinite in greatest proximity. By understanding the helper in the religious sphere can one understand the other modes of communication. Let us take our beginning in the religious dimension, seeking to share in the problematic of the enabling and facilitating process.

The religious helper's life is devoted to his ultimate concern, that which is immutable, absolute, and the source of all created things. He calls that to which his concern is directed the "eternal," not because it is timeless or of infinite duration, for of this he has no experience, but because in him is awakened an apprehension of the "timelessness of existence."[12] The helper apprehends the eternal not as an emptying or halting of time but as those moments in which the historical quality of experience, the eventfulness of moments, reaches an extreme penetration of meaning, announcing a fullness toward which temporal becoming directs itself. For the religious individual life is experienced as a process reaching toward a fulfillment rather than a termination. The particular characteristic of the Christian cosmology is that the coming of Jesus is a historical moment originating the possibility of new life through the authentication that man and God have become mediated and related.

The theological ground that enters decisively into the perspective of the Christian helper, and referring specifically to Kierkegaard, is the conception that individual development contains an authentic motive that compels it toward the futurity of being, a motive which though exercised by virtue of a finite freedom and therefore rooted in personal history may nevertheless attain to a meeting with that which is bestowed in love, eternal happiness. It is paradoxical that what a man should strive for and seek passage to apparently holds itself apart from the claims of a temporal process. But this paradox, once entered into, has the effect of catching the individual and preventing him from slipping back into an earlier mode of resolution. The aesthetical has its sensuous immediacy, the ethical has its absolutes, but the rigor of the eternal requires a trust that seems more than human, shaking the will and confounding reason. Faith is the expectation of an eternal outcome to a temporal process. It is the expectation that serves as the standard of self-development by relating the abiding to the transitory. His trusting ability to see "eventfully" is an expression of the helper's faith. He exercises his faith as a helper by calling up the eternal in every event or by making the individuals with whom he shares concern aware of the fulness of meaning which the temporality of becoming manifests.

The religious helper does not mediate between others and the Divine, rather his role is to facilitate the possibility of a continuity between seemingly incommensurable moments or aspects of experience. The discontinuities of experience wherein the individual releases himself to the act of giving beyond his inclination to give, that which Kierkegaard calls the "leap"—these advances of meaning toward fulfillment can be facilitated by the helper who introduces the aspect of continuity into the situation of discontinuity. The language of the stages of existence is one such act introducing continuity into the situation of incommensurability of meanings. The three modes of indirect communication in the dialectic of discourse strive to introduce the element of continuity into experience such that they may become whole and seen in their fullness, their consequentiality.

"The eternal is the factor of continuity,"[13] which enables the individual to experience the transition or leap, which is a "breach of continuity."[14] The facilitating dialectic of indirect discourse disclosed through the language of the stages calls up this continuity by evolving a situation of impasse or a discontinuity of meaning, a paradox or an irony. The ultimate impasse, which the religious discourse reveals, is the resistance to the Christian imperative: "Thou shalt love thy neighbor as thyself." The strangeness of this command is its call for a caring that becomes increasingly more intensive and demanding as the other, the neighbor, is experienced as unlike oneself. The relating of unlikeness in care is the extremest form of discontinuity which individuals encounter. It is the final clue to the appropriation process and proficiency of being which is human development.

The element of care which distinguishes the Christian concept and experience of love from the Greek *eros* is the universal dimension that gives Christianity its position of incompleteness in relationship to the task of fullness. This universality of task prevents Christianity from growing in upon itself. When Christianity becomes exclusive it betrays its own eternality. Yet, that such acts of exclusion have occurred in history, as they have in other religions, must be recognized. The inclusiveness of care, the universal Christian principle, is the built-in corrective to divergences in the history of the Church. Kierkegaard moves out from this essential Christian dimension into the activities of stages and spheres. The stages, when given the status of categories, illustrate the penetrability of experience and point to the eternal. They are oriented by it if they remain open to its claim.

What a religious helper does is serve this openness. The particular mode of serving and facilitating the openness of being to the eternal was, for Kierkegaard, the establishing of meaningful historicity as the context of continuity in the daily Christian world and as the link between Christianity and other forms of religious expression. He saw Socrates as the embodiment and beginning of the revealed helper in the sacred but non-Christian dimension: the humanistic. Socrates and Christ became the two turning points of history. The synchronism between them unfolds the dual dynamics of continuity in the humanistic and divine dimensions.

10.

The Limits of Language

The most encompassing perspective through which to approach Kierkegaard as educator is as religious thinker. He admonishes us to remember this when, toward the end of his authorship, he attempts to clarify his "point of view" as first, last, and always, essentially Christian.[1] From this point of view all the works of the authorship belong to a vast design having the same objective: to enable the reader to move steadily closer to Christianity. As far as the authorship goes, this movement toward Christianity takes place essentially through language that makes the appropriation of religious knowledge possible in the medium of thought. Kierkegaard's language takes its shape through a dialectic of communication. By placing himself in the situation of the reader, and by careful attention to the interaction of elements in communication—its content, mode, the recipient, and the speaker—he undertakes to illuminate the steps in the individual's becoming a Christian, steps in the process of interiorization.

Kierkegaard has the generosity of acknowledging that no one can take the steps of inward deepening except each singular individual. The language corresponding to this truth of process would, therefore, need to reflect acts of human becoming rather than final results. The speaker would share a process rather than communicate as if from the side of the accomplishment. This is why Kierkegaard would disclaim the role of teacher, because, for him, to teach has connotations of positioning oneself on the side of finality and of communicating results. Teaching, thus understood, is inconsistent with the truth of human being as self-becoming and with the ever unfinished, because always yet.to be lived, truth of becoming a Christian.

If we persist in calling Kierkegaard educator it is because his discourse reflects the difficulties of becoming a complete person and because he shows that the difficulty of the process is not the problem itself but rather that our difficulties demarcate a process. If we persist in calling Kierkegaard an educative thinker, it is because his reflective language testifies to passage from complexity to simplicity—reflection being not so much a matter of acquiring knowledge, as the appropriation process through which one finds the simple (*enkelte*) thoughts that make one whole or singular (*enkelte*).

All the modes of communication which comprise Kierkegaard's art of enabling communication lead to a fundamental use of language intended to clarify the foundation and source of human becoming. The special term qualifying the religious thinker's discourse is the "upbuilding" or "edifying" (*det opbyggelige*). While such a religious term may seem to take us far beyond the realm ordinarily belonging to education, we cannot help but focus our attention upon the ultimate design of Kierkegaard's educative language as one of building up, of constructing the possibility of appropriation of ultimate human striving. Our assumption is that even though the "upbuilding discourse" strains the dimensions of what we ordinarily mean by education, that tension will help to discover the foundations upon which the educative is built up—not only in Kierkegaard's language but in acts of speech aiming to enable processes of self-becoming, in the language of helpers in general.

By exploring the language of edification we are also exploring the limits of language. If the speaker cannot take steps for the recipient, neither can his language communicate what can only be done in silence, only in the stillness that makes authentic hearing possible. Silence becomes synonomous with inwardness; and Kierkegaard's art of communication, one in which the author is able to remain silent about that which cannot be spoken. But certainly there are other limits of language, other silences that involve cutting oneself off from communicating and, mirrored in these limits of language, refusing to respond to what calls out in personal address. This difference must be kept in mind.

As part of the upbuilding process, Kierkegaard makes efforts to point out limits of language and of speech by drawing the reader to recognition of the role of language and communication. Often, in the midst of unfolding some particular aspect of human becoming, he will pause to reflect on the difficulty of communicating something that could make a decisive difference in a person's life, as if asking, "How can this life transformation be spoken about transformatively?" The limits of communication reveal the limits of education; not so much by virtue of what is said, but by how speaking conditions the occasion and structures the event of education, an education aimed to awaken possibility.

The kind of awakening education which the issue of communication ultimately turns upon directs itself to the uplifting of the human spirit. It is an "edifying" education that concerns Kierkegaard as a religious author. Already at the end of *Either/Or* we have heard the phrase, "Only the truth that edifies is truth for you." It would be true to say, as was the case with Parson c's sermon, that the edifying concerns the difficulty of movement in the direction of the religious, the difficult path to Christianity. "Man's highest perfection is to need God," proclaims Kierkegaard in his *Edifying Discourses*.[2] To need God is to discover the limits of perfecting one's own nature as an immanent process and to turn toward the possibility of the transcendent. Yes, someone might say, but this is a religious matter of concern to the minister and his congregation or an individual and his relationship to God. How can such talk about edification apply to the context of an ethical educator such as Judge William, or in the more mundane problems of human relationships, or when people counsel one another?

However finite are the goals of more ordinary discourse, there is always an ideal, a paradigm of the highest possibilities of communication. Our concern here is to explore this contrast between the ordinary and the extraordinary in educative language as the contrast between common and edifying discourse. Kierkegaard himself has something like this in mind when he contrasts the language of Christianity with more ordinary speech.

> The Christian language uses the same words we men use, and in that respect desires no change. But it uses them qualitatively different from the way we use them; it uses the words inversely, for Christianity makes manifest one sphere more or a higher sphere than the one in which we men naturally live, and in this sphere ordinary human language is reflected inversely.[3]

A qualitatively different use of language is exemplified for Kierkegaard in the phrase, "that to lose the earthly is a gain, that to possess it is a loss." Ordinary use of "loss and gain" are inverted here in what seem like contradictions but which in actual life function more as paradoxes of existence: to lose is to gain, to possess is to lose.

The qualitatively different use of language must, for Christianity, be accompanied by a qualitative change in awareness. And such radical alteration of human awareness as this inversion of ordinary meaning is, in fact, embodied in Biblical and New Testament forms of discourse such as parables, proverbs, and paradoxes. The two spheres, the higher and lower or extraordinary and ordinary language, reflect into one another as infinite and finite spheres of human experience. If these two spheres were completely separate from one another, then there would be neither passage from one to the other nor communication across their boundaries. The theory advanced here is that they are not separated by degrees, as, for instance, in the extended meaning or use a word might have, but by a corresponding alteration of awareness which is not merely heightened but fundamentally transformed, so that the world named by language becomes a transformed one. By changing the point of reference upon which the perspective of ordinary language rests, that language suddenly takes on new meaning. Particularly through contrast with the world of assumed language, religious language deepens the individual's realization of his situation. One way in which this happens is in the moment of a person's recognition of his mortality, which qualitatively transforms his experience of time and personal history. Another, for Kierkegaard, is "sin-consciousness," an individual's experience of imperfection and fallibility before God. To sin-consciousness comes the realization of a higher possibility than is "natural" for man, the 'possibility of new life and of grace. Generally, we could say that for Kierkegaard these transformations involve a dramatic alteration of a person's relationship to time and its significance.

One of the functions of Kierkegaard's own language is to be consistent with this transformation, through language, to religious consciousness, either by indirect communication, which points to but does not posit the way, or by direct discourse, in which the narrator is a witness to his own process of religious awakening—as is the case in Kierkegaard's *Christian Discourses*. The art of Kierkegaard's educative language in this respect depends upon his never speaking as "from above." He may point to a process that stands transcendently related to the situation of the reader or even related as an ideal for himself, but the final posture of the spiritual master who has attained divine wisdom is never taken. This had lead some scholars to wonder whether Kierkegaard ever reached such knowledge. Our particular concern here is not with this issue as such, but with the formulation Kierkegaard offers and enacts in language of the relationship between the two spheres and the dynamic process of crossing the boundary from one to the other.

Passage across the threshold of meaning remains problematic for Kierkegaard as an edifying author whose own language is supremely poetical, exercising aesthetically an art of discourse while serving a language of the spirit. Is there not a problem here of Kierkegaard's poetic language overshadowing the language of the spirit, i.e., Christian Scripture? How transparent and yet helpful can language become? How far can Kierkegaard take us or enable us to go toward completing the process of human becoming? Our approach to the relationship between the two spheres—the finite and infinite, limit and unlimit—will focus upon the form of intermediacy which joins their corresponding languages, the role of metaphor in Kierkegaard. To gain passage from aesthetic to religious language and to discover their interrelationship, we begin by finding a first formulation of problems of passage between two adjacent spheres qualitatively separated from one another in the language of *Either/Or*'s A. Some will consider it a Kierkegaardian heresy to place the aesthete and that first aesthetic work side by side with Kierkegaard's reflections on edifying language in his ethico-religious "Discourse in the Form of Christian Reflections," in *Works of Love* (1847). We shall take that risk in endeavoring to show how A's struggle with passage from the immediacy of the aesthetic, life lived in feeling and mood, to the life of ethical reflectivity, life lived in decision, establishes a central metaphor of language limits. This metaphor serves as an analogy to Kierkegaard's two spheres and the passage from first (aesthetic) to the "second immediacy" of an edified (religious) awareness, a passage whereby limits of language become a language of limits.

A's language embodies limits in portraying the very movements of his experiences. He actually comes to address these limits explicitly in some reflections on Mozart's opera *Don Juan*. But first let us examine a piece of A's linguistic con-

sciousness given in one of the diapsalmata or "refrains" with
which *Either/Or* begins.

> The sun shines into my room bright and beautiful, the
> window is open in the next room; on the street all is
> quiet, it is a Sunday afternoon. Outside the window, I
> clearly hear a lark pour forth its song in a neighbor's
> garden, where the pretty maiden lives. Far away in a dis-
> tant street I hear a man crying shrimp. The air is so
> warm, and yet the whole town seems dead.—Then I
> think of my youth and of my first love—when the long-
> ing of desire was strong. Now I long only for my first
> longing. What is youth, A dream. What is love? The
> substance of a dream.[4]

This little vignette, which is rather less poignant at first
reading than some of the other diapsalmata, is a perfect crys-
tallization of the relationship between language and life disposition in the world of A. In it, the limits encountered by the
speaker are mirrored in the limits of his language. A Sunday
afternoon in nineteenth century Copenhagen must have
been, as it remains today (apart from the tourist season), a
time when friends and family collect indoors while outside is
stillness and repose. But the last day of this week finds the
solitary speaker in a moment of isolation when everything
seems to have come to an end. As the sunlight pours into the
space of his room, sounds from the outside draw his inward
reflection through a set of frames of experience, each containing and adding to the previous impression, until the buildup
reaches consummation in the mood of melancholy. The narrator passes through room, window, garden, street, and
town to the memory of a period of life, to a dream. An irrep-
arable sense of loss terminates the particular present moment
and directs it to the past. There can be no future, no hope.
The present is contained by the past and memory temptingly
offers the solace of regained innocence in the wistful wisdom
that all is illusion, the inventions of dreams. What is it that
animates this static picture of immediacy? The reader is car-

ried along with the speaker out of a room, through a window, into a garden where he reaches the pretty maiden. Abruptly, distance is invoked and the scene shifts from the visual to the auditory with the cry, "shrimps!" We are surprised by the juxtaposition of ideality expressed in the lark's song—the lyrical sound of the garden and the innocent maiden—followed by the harsher realities of experience called up in the distant vendor's shouting of the word shrimps. The linking of the lark's song and the cry, "shrimps!" creates a contrast through the apposition of sounds. The word shrimp cried in the distance limits the song of the lark and turns the speaker around to himself. By means of association, he reaches through the static frame, "the whole town seems dead," to another time interior to this Sunday afternoon, to the time of past youth. The contrast of sounds leads him to a moment of pristine immediacy: first love. But again, as in the external movement into the garden of the maiden, he abruptly turns from the object of desire and, reaching back along its path, ends by replacing the object of desire with himself. He reaches himself reaching out and, taking hold of himself, he comes to the inverted reflection: "What is youth? A dream."

In his own diary, Kierkegaard rather melodramatically portrays the aesthete, A, caught in the situation of unreflective despair. He cannot risk the attachment to what is beyond himself for fear of self-loss. To prevent this he replaces the object of desire by an objectless emotion; he embraces himself. Still, the demand of love really remains unanswered. And because it is unanswered it can no longer be heard. Instead of passing through melancholy to what might lie on the other side, reflection is avoided in the instant of colliding sounds. The speaker's voice identifies with itself. The inverted reach of language entraps its own reflected light, the lively (*livligt*) sunlight enters a space emptied of time where the timelessness of youth is not a memory but an illusion of transcendency. The aesthete's language operates as a one-way mirror: he observes himself reflected in it and through it he can be observed, but he cannot see beyond his own image. At best, the reader may be able to see himself in the speaker's language, as Kierkegaard attempted to place the discourse in the aesthetic immediacy (paganism) of the reader. The shape of the discourse reveals A's life disposition. It reflects A's bounded awareness and fundamental passivity, just as a coincidence of sounds in the external world becomes a metaphor for an inner world in which A is unwilling to relinquish the immediacy of feeling. The juxtaposition of lark's song and "shrimp!" becomes a metaphor of limit.

The relationship between opposing qualities of sound in this diapsalm causes A to close down upon his own possibilities rather than to reach an awareness that might enable him to move beyond his melancholy. Many of the diapsalmata have this sort of linguistic twist where, encountering a contradiction or impasse, the discourse folds back on itself. His is a language that does not want any of its content to escape to the freedom of possibility. This is nicely summed up in another diapsalm. "I have but one friend, Echo; and why is Echo my friend? Because I love my sorrow, and Echo does not take it from me."[5] Like the auditory metaphor of limit, the personification of Echo implies acts of calling out within closed spaces. But, while A is apparently entrapped by echoes from the past, he deifies sound, rather than sight, as the supreme form of human sensibility. The fleeting immediacy of sound invites the imagination to transcend the rational order of a spatial-visual world in fathoming the depths of the mysterious self. Precisely this tendency of the nineteenth century romantic sensibility to deify sound in the form of music accounts for A's interest in the problem of language limits, which becomes explicit in his reflections on aesthetic theory. Going beyond being a victim of an auditory metaphor, A finds the relationship between language (reflection) and music (immediacy) an opportunity to formulate an aesthetic theory that is also a personal one. To the caricatured use of the term "aesthetic" is conjoined its more traditional meaning as the "science of the beautiful." These two meanings of aesthetic become paralleled in a discussion of the ideality of music in A's essay on "The Immediate Stages of the Erotic or the Musical Erotic." To appreciate A's discourse on music, where the problem of language limits is reformulated, it will be helpful to become familiar with the aesthetic theory then in predominance and no doubt at the back of A's mind. A very brief mention of Hegel's theory of aesthetics will be an invaluable guide to much of what follows.

For Hegel, art was a mode for representing the highest ideals in sensuous form. The ancient Greeks, he believed, reached the point of perfection in achieving the unity of sensuous figure and spiritual ideal in their sculpture. But with the advent of Christianity, mind broke the fetters of abstract naturalism and reconceived itself as infinite subjectivity, as absolute Spirit. The relationship of adequacy of content to form was, says Hegel, forever sundered. The infinite inwardness of this new human consciousness could never again be given a sensuous form to which, as content, it would not be transcendent. That form of art in which a pure and limitless content would always be seeking to overreach any particular sensuous form was Romantic art, which, for Hegel, had its inception with the coming into being of Christian consciousness. Romantic art called for a new understanding of the role of form. This developed in the transition from spatially articulated forms such as architecture and sculpture to those utilizing temporal articulation such as music and poetry. In fact, for Hegel, music, which becomes so important for Christianity, marked the despatialization of the sensuous in its aesthetic idealization. The spatiality of the sculpted or painted image was collapsed into a point of sound in time, more in accordance with the inward truth of Spirit which had become essentially nonsensuous. Nevertheless, for Hegel, however far art might reach in mediating the opposition between the spiritual and the sensuous, the infinite and the finite, it would still only be able to bring into consciousness and expression the relatively divine meaning of things. It was left to reflection, thinking, indeed to philosophy to reach an absolute accordance with Being. Only the philosopher would be able to think the truth of the whole—the entire development of thought in coming to think itself as absolute Spirit.[6]

A, in wistful appreciation of Hegel's aesthetic theory, undertakes to depict the birth of consciousness in its pristine immediacy by finding in Mozart's opera, *Don Juan*, absolute and inseparable union between content and form embodying the purest expression of desire. In doing so he reverses Hegelian categories by making a romantic piece of art a "classic" one, but inversely he makes his situation of reflecting on this classic, a romantic one. His phenomenological account of stages of immediate consciousness (desire) dresses Hegel's abstract language in the erotic costume of *Don Juan*. For A, Mozart has embodied the ideal of sensuous immediacy in his operatic form. There, character, language, and music comprise an inextricable unity. He undertakes to participate in that union and communicate his enthusiasm for the inner mystery of the opera. But he discovers that, lacking the musician's language of immediacy, he must content himself with the use of a reflective language to gain an intuition of the whole. A finds, however, that he remains standing on the outside of Mozart's perfect aesthetic union.

There may be a way of speaking or writing where this obstacle is overcome, but for the moment A confronts the unbridgeable separation between music and language. And unlike Hegel, in what amounts to being a parody of his aesthetic theory, A finds that music lets us hear what conscious reflective thinking can never say, even to itself. Hearing, for A, bears out Victor Eremita's editorial observation that what is auditory often reveals the distinction between two worlds of experience, the inner and outer, between an illusory world of appearances and one of true feelings. Seeing can involve deceiving, but in listening we more readily detect the inward reference of voice to speaker's reality. As the ultimate expression of the immediate, sensuous dimension, music when masterfully handled by the genius of Mozart, provides a direct experience of what otherwise must remain silent. Music lets one hear what could otherwise not be heard or spoken; music "sounds" the unsayable, as the argument goes, because it is the perfect medium for that which is illusive to reflection, for moods that are so comprehensive that no distinct object can be separated out from them. Music allows us to reach the heart of kinds of experience which language, in its reflective aspects, cannot allow, because as soon as language begins to name things (even moods) it alters their status through mediation.

Limit and unlimit are brought to paradoxical proximity in a parable of "two kingdoms" where language (finite reflection) and music (infinite immediacy) join limits at a common frontier. Here A situates himself in his task of writing about Don Juan and desire.

> If I imagined two kingdoms adjoining one another, with one of which I was fairly well acquainted, and altogether unfamiliar with the other, and I was not allowed to enter the unknown realm, however much I desired to do so, I should still be able to form some conception of its nature. I could go to the limits of the kingdom with which I was acquainted and follow its boundaries, and as I did so, I should in this way describe the boundaries of this unknown country, and thus without ever having set foot in it, obtain a general conception of it.[7]

A pictures himself an "initiate at the gates," he seeks passage, he has expectations of a revelation, but he cannot find the means to cross over. Unable to find the means, he will go to extremes in mapping the unknown but desirable territory —indeed, the province of desire itself, which he later calls the "kingdom of sin." Language, because it is fettered by temporal reflection, stands impotently before music's "daemonic" domain—music, which has "an element of time in itself, but does not take place in time." Not that language as a medium lacks its own perfection; language most perfectly expresses reflections and their ultimate consummation in ideas. Language is the spiritually qualified kingdom, says A, tipping his comic hat toward the Hegelians. Hence, these media should be understood as countries, which, though bordering one another, are understood to have autonomy and sovereignty. Which is the superior? That is an issue for the ethical man to judge.

Returning to A's mapping, we see him proceed through the following circumnavigations. Move imaginatively, says A to the furthest reaches from music in language and you arrive at prose. Notice that even in prose one finds the "sonorous structure" or "oratorical discourse." Move to poetry and you find the structure of verse, rhyme, in fact language itself becoming lyrical. Go in the opposite direction, downward through prose interpenetrated by conceptualization, until you come to the child's first babbling syllable (what we now call a phoneme), again the musical. The cartographer's conclusion: "music everywhere limits language." A's effort to circumscribe music produces one potentially fruitful result: the limits of language become transformed into a language of limit. This is important, asserts A, because now he can proceed maieutically to say the unsayable, to exercise a mode of "lyrical thought" which will "worry into breaking forth" the absolute subject of music: "force, life, movement, constant unrest, perpetual succession." Behold, music sounds! Or does it? Perhaps we ought to consult our map again.

A's goal is to let the sensuous genius of Mozart's *Don Juan* "be heard." He will not, cannot, say it. But having contracted the limits of his situation, having conjoined, as only irony can conjoin, the *an sich* and the *fur sich*, he will repeat the act of bordering together what stand as unlike to each other, even as known and unknown. Just as lark's song and "shrimp!" create a dialectical world of infinite/finite complexity, so language and music or their contents, reflection and desire, reconstitute this world of limit situations. The language of limit "worries forth" (*aengste frem*) by a gentle but persistent shaking at the throat where we await either song or statement. And while our expectations increase, the question arises: With what adequacy, to what extent, how does language mirror force, life, movement, constant unrest? What is the relationship between reflective language (thinking, even if lyrical) and life (existence)? A dismisses any effort to establish an isomorphic relationship between his language and Mozart's sensuous genius. Instead, he assures us of the unlikeness through a juxtaposition, inviting us to move with him along the limits of boundary. We must return to this questioning of the relationship of philosophy to life, as Kierkegaard would return to it over and over.

If A's parable of the two kingdoms is structurally like a metaphor, he places himself into a metaphorical posture by attempting to reach through the relation of familiar and strange to the *recreation of possibility*. He does not himself cross the threshold to which he brings the reader. Instead, he dwells in what we might think of as an "intra meta-metaphor zone," one that seems only to refer back to itself. Significantly, A explicitly returns to the problem of metaphor (*billeder*, literally, "pictures") in a final effort to break through both to music's secret kingdom and to the reader. While earlier he sought to worry forth (*aengste frem*) the essence of Mozart's *Don Juan*, now he undertakes to speak about Don Juan's essential energy as itself "substantial dread" (*angest*). And it is this, says A, which will justify the use of a form of language he usually distrusts, namely, metaphorical language or figures of speech (*billedsprög*). With these "figures" A hopes to "touch his reader" and put himself in touch with Don Juan's erotic desire and his dark dread.

A's problem with language becomes inextricably entangled with Don Juan's seduction complex, a problem A shares with the reader but of which the Don remains forever unaware. A's lyrical efforts to visualize music that evokes the dark side of Don Juan's mythical existence cannot be reproduced here. It consists of blackness and a horizon intermittently illuminated by lightening: Don Juan at a limit. His sexual proclivities, the desire for conquest and the ecstatic fulfillment of self-satisfaction, always conclude with an abrupt turn away from possibilities of lingering possession of the seduced. Don Juan must remain the beloved-lover. He loves and lives to love as A in the diapsalm yearns to yearn. In Don Juan's desiring, A reproduces his own self-reaching and the limit of his reach, which is fear of possession and especially of the reciprocal being possessed. Don Juan is nothing but desire and is therefore self-complete; what completes him is that which contains him, dread, fear of an unknown domain that may or may not hold the key to his quest.

As midwife of desire, A puts the reader in touch with desire. The reader hears in A's language himself desiring. Reflection falls equally on reader and author, and the language of limit, in the aesthetic dialectic of communication, reaches the anticipation of possibility.

The representative voice of aesthetic discourse goes to extremes of language when he reaches out for metaphors. A locates himself in a metaphorical quandary: the sensuous erotic and the spiritually reflective are everywhere coterminous, as the worlds of sexuality and speculation are everywhere points of passage into one another if the vehicle of transcendence can be found. But how can the limits of language serve a content that is always outreaching itself? Is there a form of speech that, unlike A's, not merely circumscribes but participates in that which it signifies?

This journey to the limiting boundaries of language provides an analogy for the situation of the religious author whose aim is to enable the reader to cross limits of language into the kingdom, not of music's first immediacy, but of the "second immediacy" of spiritual understanding. We have explored several indirect forms of discourse which serve to facilitate a qualitative transformation in life disposition. Irony and humor are the primary modes of discourse which serve to bridge from the aesthetic to the ethical and then from the ethical to the religious life-disposition. By contrasting an infinite task to a finite means and by dramatic and conceptual emphasis on human becoming as a temporal process, these forms evoke a qualitative transformation of life perspective. The crossing of boundaries between secular and spiritual spheres of awareness has a third form of facilitation, that of love. On one side, it is human generosity in its highest form, and on the other side, God's gift of the transcendent to man. Human and divine love in the dimension of the spirit form the counterpart to A's kingdom of desire and the erotic education of the Socratic teacher which we explored in Part I. An edifying education is essentially one grounded in a conception and experience of love. The movement over thresholds of awareness is profoundly reformulated in the context of Christian ethics concerning the love of the neighbor. The discourse to which we now turn draws together the issues of communication, language, education and the limits of education in the context of love. The former aesthetic problem of metaphor's enabling the author to touch the reader is seen to parallel religious discourse, as the language of love reaches toward a loving language.

11.
The Language of Limits

The tension of contrasting form is the
measure of the intensity of inwardness.
—*Concluding Unscientific Postscript*

Kierkegaard uses the word "transfer" (*overføre*)—a literal
equivalent of the Greek *metapherein* (*pherein*, to carry;
meta, beyond) to describe language that not only conveys a
meaning but conveys speaker and recipient to a meeting or
event in which the truth of the "beyond" (whether we call it
the unknown kingdom, the eternal, the future) is disclosed.[1]
The helper's language is essentially metaphorical because it
points to a hiddenness, bringing unlikeness into proximity,
and because it reveals the nature of the power in which the
helper takes his stand. Transferred speaking aims to establish
a continuity between unlikenesses: between eternal and temporal existence, between the familiar and the strange, between the I and Thou where the Thou is the single witness—
the other who dwells nearby, the neighbor for whom one's
caring is beyond the immediacy of inclination or preference
—and the Thou is the Divine Presence addressing the recipient as *Du* in the paradoxical intimacy of obedience to one's
own highest life principle.

In *Works of Love* (*Kjerlighedens Gjerninger*, 1848), word
and deed are drawn together as like and unlike, as neighbors.
The deed that conveys love but does not let itself become
mistaken as its source shows love as a gift to mankind, one
"which never arose in any man's heart."[2] The dialectic has

broken with the immanent and turns to a consideration of the deeds that prepare the recipient for grace. But the dialectic does not let go of the fact that these deeds are human and transpire between man and man. The particular art of religious discourse which Kierkegaard describes here is the appropriation process that is the event of the recipient opening himself to the words of Scripture. More broadly considered, Kierkegaard portrays religious devotion and human care as they intersect in acts that facilitate a realization of how man and God, man and man, how the lover, the beloved, and the neighbor belong to one another.

Works of Love gives a first impression of a series of sermons. One soon finds that its relationship to the reader is to "awaken" rather than persuade. Knowledge of the Divine is not presupposed but rather called up or aroused. These are "Christian reflections" through which the temporal and eternal are each weighed against the other. He who weighs the two magnitudes is himself a third magnitude striving to unite the absolute lightness of the eternal and the absolute heaviness of the temporal. A discourse on Christian ethics has then the problem of making the light heavy and the heavy correspondingly light. Language will be called upon to serve as a double witness: to take up the case from both sides, or to let the two sides of itself become present to each other. What kind of language confirms the inner dialogue of man's dual nature, maintaining its connectedness while remaining faithful to the paradox of unification? Man, the third magnitude, is the spoken metaphor that unites and separates in the same breath.

What is the situation and what the condition for metaphorical utterances? A transformation is undertaken, just as a metamorphosis of self was proposed to A. The present focus of the dialectics of religious discourse does not, in this instance, dwell upon the inherent powers of the self, the will, or man's enduring suffering—his passion. The decisive act is the response that goes out to meet the possibility conveyed by certain scriptural phrases. We are no longer concerned with a single instantaneous movement from stage to stage. It is rather the modulation of the human duality, brought to the correct intensity, that enables the interaction of the temporal and eternal to become visible. Kierkegaard is focusing upon the power of the Word, the *logos*, to make us visible to ourselves. But it is his own language that serves as the background for its effect. His language, which is to a significant degree poetical, aims to facilitate this meeting of the human spirit with the *logos*. The effort is paradoxical since the success of his own art would mean the overshadowing of divine language. Yet he finds that he must speak, that he must take the chance that the sensuous medium of language may conceal that which is purely spirit. Even though his subject is Christian ethics, Kierkegaard's problem lies in the meeting of the aesthetical and the religious. It is nothing less than the justification of a lifetime of work undertaken for the sake of the eternal. He sees that if this problem itself is not made known, that the communication's content be revealed through a realization of how it has been disclosed, then the heavy (finite) will have been mistaken for the light (infinite) and the light assumed to be heavy. The situation to which the metaphorical gives testimony is the relating of the absolutely different, the heavy and the light. And a transference is embodied in this juxtaposition, a transference from the heavy to the light —and back again. The newness of meaning comes to be born out of the juxtaposition of what were seemingly unlike though familiar elements of life. The task is not only the moment of change, the event of rebirth, but the whole long process of growing up again and growing through the patterns of a familiar world which has become strange, wondrous, become new and praiseworthy. We shall see that Kierkegaard makes his own act of speaking testify to that which it cannot contain. It is the situation in which a sensation of repeated gift-giving is experienced as a transaction in the gift of language to man. If there is something immanent in the process it is the perseverance and openness to the repetition of language which holds the power to make new over and over.

The closer words come to describing the immutable and invisible the more heavy they grow with the heightened burden of the temporal. Yet with each renewing event and with each realization, the single witness is called to praise that which comes from beyond the perimeters of language.

Only the language of love can bring the opposites, heavy and light, together. It is acts of love which unite the unequal through extraordinary understanding. The understanding confines itself to that which can be resolved by reason. Something more is called for than common understanding. There is an unreasonable demand which asks us to be more than human. This unjust demand requires us to be equal to the situation in which something "essentially indescribable" is made known to us.[3] To become more than human would require superhuman assistance. And a language that would testify to a divine feat, so as to facilitate that miracle, would itself need to become an "extraordinary" kind of speaking. It is just this kind of extraordinary speaking which Kierkegaard celebrates as the word of Scripture. In doing so he also celebrates his own language, which connects itself to the tradition of the Apostles. The language of ultimate help is then the language that conveys divine assistance. It is a language that requires faith for its appropriation. Faith makes the recipient equal to the situation of a divine gift, God's love. It is a gift that calls for praise and continuation, for the gift cannot be kept to oneself.

When Kierkegaard, in the first part of *Works of Love*, introduces Matthew's testimony of the divine command, "Thou shalt love thy neighbor as thyself," he pronounces a radical shift in orientation from the focus on individual inwardness to a concern for human development as it manifests itself in the community of man. The autonomy of an inward building process is beckoned outward; not toward things of material significance, but toward the common life shared with others—with those who are "nearby," with strangers. The neighbor and the self are the new characters of development. They belong to one another by virtue of a gift of love which belongs to neither the one nor the other singly. The divine command does not rest in a realm of otherworldly ideals. Kierkegaard derives a dramatic reversal of the commonly held assumption about emotion and feeling in the context of Matthew's message.

A friend, the beloved, one's child, a stranger has occasion to speak in such a way that an emotion, a strong feeling is aroused in us. Is not this feeling our personal property? Is it not for us to choose when, where, and how to give a response to the other? Ordinarily we assume that our development is a personal matter, for which we claim a private right. But the words of Matthew reveal that self-development is not only for oneself but for others. We are for others in our development. Kierkegaard intimates the work of love when he says that precisely because the emotion was evoked by the other it belongs to the other, "since in the emotion you belong to him who moves you and makes you conscious of belonging to him."[4]

The work of love is that which makes us conscious of belonging to the other, whether the other is a neighbor, an enemy, or the Divine Presence—even possibly, though Kierkegaard does not say so explicitly, when the other is an estranged or rejected part of ourselves. "You belong to him who moves you," says Kierkegaard, not only to what is said but to the person present in the communication. Is this an example of indirect communication? As part of a written expression indirect communication involves something different. But it is related if we understand that to respond from ourselves to the person who spoke in the statement that moved us, is to respond not simply from motives that separate identities, but to answer the mover and the movement in the communication. When response is directed more toward how a person comes across, to that which moves us, to how we belong to the other, then the response that shares a process can easily be seen as indirect in contrast to conventional modes. But the indirect response may in fact be the most intimate one because it refers not to one or the other but to that which is common for both.

What takes place in language is not our possession, for

additional to what is said, the speaking act calls for a meeting in language, a meeting in a commonly shared dimension of time. It is only by this act of letting language speak without interposing our notions of rights to reticence that the true belonging to one another is discoverable. If the response is saved, held for alteration, hoarded or hidden for one reason or another, then the leaves of Luke's tree which whisper care and love will be eaten up, wither, and no fruit will be born.[5]

Here then is the neighbor, whose presence is a testimony to the trueness of speaking and whose unlikeness comes as a test to the equality that is love's essential quality when love is fruitful and increases in the presence of strangers, rather than shrinking and hiding itself away in private intimacies. Language's capacity for metaphor is like love's capacity in the presence of the unlikely object of love, the neighbor: they both become fruitful and enriched and renewing through the encounter with the different and the strange.

The structural situation advanced in Part One of *Works of Love* prepares us for the second part, where Kierkegaard takes as a point of departure the distinction between knowledge (*kundskab*) and love (*kjerlighed*) that is found in St. Paul's 1 Corinthians 8 and 13. In this context Kierkegaard describes a twofold transformation in the concept of the eternal, where the first is Socratic and the second, Christian. The first transformation involves a turning toward the subject. It is an ethical turning that emphasizes one's duty to be faithful to one's self through openness toward the appropriation of divine commands. The first transformation is self-continuity's eternality, the autonomy of the person, which, in *Either/Or*, was called his "eternal validity." But now there comes a second transformation: in the first, rebirth and the moment of impregnation is decisive; in the second, the seasons of the tree of Luke with its fruit and leaves introduces generations of development and repeated renewals. The eternal within the historical characterizes the second, the Christian principle of the eternal. The eternal within the historical is the beckoning agent of human destiny.

Everything that was given to the subject is now to be activated. The real is to become realized, the actual to become actualized, and love—love is to become a deed, an act of language. The need to be loved must grow into the need to love: everything that has been received as a precious gift is now to be exercised faithfully. The second eternality is the emergence toward the Thou in whom one discovers a common future; just as metaphor points to the fulfillment of new meanings by establishing a bridge over the discontinuity of old ones.

The "third man of equality," the neighbor, stands vividly in the place that forms the triangularity of love.[6] Socrates speaks of eros whose dual-nature, mortal and immortal, gives him (Eros) the property of being a messenger between man and his gods (*Symposium*); and so the neighbor symbolizes and evokes the nature of a love that testifies to the Divine. The infinity of love is its inclusiveness, by which it makes equals from unequals. So the presence of the neighbor in the triad of love evokes the possibility of love's infinity.

Rather than being friends or lovers, the neighbors are beside one another with all their differences. Friends and lovers are like oneself already, or we discover a likeness in them to us, we incline toward them. This is self-love in the sense that what we love is ultimately the sameness between us. But self-love is released and grows when it can include others—the third member, "the first Thou," whose presence is the presence of love itself, or the capacity of love to be inclusive and make equal. Thus, says Kierkegaard, the neighbor provides opportunity for the discovery that to love one's neighbor is to see God as the middle term.[7]

To love oneself as one loves one's neighbor, is this not metaphorical, are we not transferred to an unexpected place to approach an unexpected likeness? Neighbor and self become strange in this command, a command to a Thou from a Thou, and a command that says "shall" because the unfulfilled is ever present and ever to be fulfilled. The language of Scripture is Kierkegaard's ultimate help and the human helper's relation to it is one of humility. His faithfulness to the potentially helping language of Scripture makes the helper the facilitator while limiting his authority as a source of help; for after all, the helper is also only a neighbor.

In the following part of this section we turn to the second half of *Works of Love* and, particularly, to Kierkegaard's conception of language which transfers speaker and listener to a meeting, the language of Scripture which transfers individuals from the known to the unknown kingdom. The language of love does not tread around the outside of the eternal citadel, as A does in describing the spirituality of music, but enters in across a number of bridges. By entering into the dimensions of an extraordinary language, edifying language, we shall find the unfolding movement of the human spirit reflected in the action of religious language itself.

Kierkegaard speaks with the intent of edifying the reader, that he might be stirred into action. But he cannot resist the temptation to share with the reader the very issue of the difficulty of being an edifying author. What emerges from this is Kierkegaard's philosophy of speech and, subsequently, language. For a few puzzling pages Kierkegaard reflects on language, speech, and metaphor in such a way that a rhetoric of edification becomes an enabling communication.

Having accepted the linguistic limits of the inexpressible, Kierkegaard proceeds to set himself two further limits. He divides his readers into two groups: those who hear only what is literally said and cannot imagine that they mean more than what they literally say; and a second group who both hear and say beyond the literalness of language, even if they should be heard to utter statements otherwise identical to members of the first group. The difference between those who perceive an irony, recognize pathos and humor, in the tone of a statement, and those who do not is what is being distinguished. Kierkegaard explains this by saying that members of the second group have passed from the "sensuous-psychical" dimension of life experience to that of the "spiritual" in such a way that the former becomes a base for the latter.[8] Language for the first group (earlier stage) seems to involve the univocal identity of word and thing. But members of the second group (later stage) have passed into a realm of equivocal language, a development ushering them into the world of ambiguity, abundance of meanings, and correspondingly, a recognition of the need to interpret the speech and manner of listening of others. If the reader understands how this distinction "makes a world of difference", then he belongs on the same side of the limit as the speaker Kierkegaard. This makes the reader now, perhaps unwittingly, what Kierkegaard would call himself: a witness.[9] In this way Kierkegaard creates a limit by means of which he gets us to cross over to the side of the speaker who is also now an interpreter. Correspondingly, we are invited to cross the distinction between a world of speech in which things are simply what they are (necessity), and one in which they enter into becoming (possibility), calling us to choose, respond, and anticipate a world in process of becoming what it "ought" to be. And Kierkegaard says that the form of an ethical communication will be such that it promotes our "oughtness capability."[10]

If this first additional limit tends, by means of our becoming "witnesses," to blur an assumed distinction between author and reader—one which, by the way, must be carefully maintained in purely ethical communications, which stand apart from the "ethico-religious" ones—then the second limit that Kierkegaard imposes on himself brings sharpness and rigor to the issues of speaking and listening. Kierkegaard contends that love is already present in each person as soon as he recognizes love as a transcendent gift from the Divine. This transformation from immanent or inherent love to transcendent love parallels, for Kierkegaard, the metamorphosis of persons from the group one into the group two mentioned earlier. Crucial here is Kierkegaard's further contention that only a person who sought to undermine this capacity for participating in the gift of transcendent love would imagine a responsibility to implant it in others. Moreover, such efforts to implant love in others are really an attempt to take power and dominate. Kierkegaard cites individuals whose vocation intimately involves speaking, such as teachers, as potential transgressors of this limit.[11] But now the rigor of this presupposition must hold also for educator Kierkegaard. Pursuing the presence of love, which we remember is at the heart of Christian ethics in the teaching on the love of the neighbor, sets a rigorous limit to the form of discourse appropriate for the situation of speaker and listener where to step across this limit would mean interfering with the very capability the speaker intends to foster in the listener.

The distinction here is for Kierkegaard a paradigm case between those situations that call for teaching in the sense of directly communicating the thing to be known, and those situations that fall more properly under indirect discourse where everything depends upon the learner's or recipient's predisposition.[12] Kierkegaard then distinguishes between teaching, where there is usually little reflection upon the medium of communication, and fostering, where Kierkegaard asks us to take a second look at the word "foster," *opelsker*, that we might find in it the activity of *op-elsker*, "loving forth."

It is, therefore, not at all strange that Kierkegaard brings these limits into a form by taking for his "edifying reflections" St. Paul's statement in 1 Corinthians (8) that "knowledge puffs up, but love is edifying" (*Kundskaben opblaeser men kjerligheden opbygger*). Kierkegaard takes his stand, begins, with love. But he seeks a path to knowledge that transforms mere knowing about something into appropriate or self-knowledge. Recognizing the limits of language is an essential clue to the form in which we know ourselves.

The issue in *Works of Love* is made to turn on the word *opbygger*, edifying, and it does so for three reasons: first, because edification is at the center of Christian experience as it is conveyed by the language of Scripture; second, because edification holds the contrast between knowledge and love as that between directly and indirectly communicable experience, and Kierkegaard holds that ethics involves not a transfer of knowledge from one person (who has it) to another (who does not have it), but rather the evoking of a human capacity that belongs to everyone; and third, because the word "edify" can itself be shown to contain a field of contrast which opens metaphorically, then points symbolically, and finally reaches an occasion in which language becomes miraculous as the coming into being of God in the form of a servant.

Having invited us to join him in his presuppositions about language and love, Kierkegaard greets us with the following startling statement. "All human language, even the divine language of holy Scripture about the spiritual, is essentially transferred language."[13] Kierkegaard uses the term *overført Tale*, transferred language, where he might have used the Danish *metaphorisk*, metaphorical. In doing so, he emphasizes the significance of the original Greek *metapherein*, since *overført* means literally "carried over." He draws our attention to this linguistic act of movement by means of which certain ways of speaking actually transfer us beyond a world of limit. And he is also playing with a second sense of "transfer" which belongs to the world of bookkeeping. The bookkeeper "carries over" (*overfører*) figures of income and expenditure in order to maintain the balance in economy. In that sense, he renders an accounting, as Kierkegaard would later give an "accounting" (*Regnskabet*) of his intentions as author in *Point of View*.

By transferred language (*overført Tale*), then Kierkegaard is suggesting to those of us who are members of his "second group" a theory of metaphorical utterance. And he will find in the word "edify" (*opbygge*) itself the instantiation of such language in the form of a "transferred term." In order to better appreciate what is to follow, we might recall Philip Wheelwright's identification of "diaphor" as a type of metaphor created through the comparison between a familiar and a less familiar term, where the comparison evokes a contrast enabling us to "reach through" the comparison to the discovery of new meaning.[14] It is precisely this reaching through or beyond that Kierkegaard has in mind. And it is precisely the contrast between the familiar and the strange that enables us to do this.

Kierkegaard finds transformative limits of language, limits that not only point beyond language to what is ultimately ineffable, but also sometimes produce that transparency that shows us the structure of our very efforts to speak. He makes an effort to show, by the existence of language, a transparency in which one becomes conscious of one's own situation as a speaker. This reflective transparency Kierkegaard calls "thinking." And this thinking is such that it frequently brings the thinker to a halt in the form of a paradox. It is precisely the paradox's capacity to release the thinker from the captivity of his own thoughts that Kierkegaard points to. Such a paradoxical situation is found in language, the finite medium, when we try to express something essentially "spiritual," of the infinite domain. The limits of language for Kierkegaard are, in fact, primarily communicative ones, i.e., limits of speech. But these limits go back to the fact of language's finitude. Still, for Kierkegaard, there is a border region where fact and value meet. And Kierkegaard finds in metaphor language's capacity to transfer speakers and listeners to a threshold of meaning.

Kierkegaard takes the word *opbygge* as a paradigmatic instance of a transferred term, a term whose metaphorical qualities contribute to the making of a "transferred language" and, therefore, to a language that itself has the power to educate by initiating us into the mysteries of speech. These mysteries are found in the limits to which language brings us, enabling us to go—however silently—into a limitless world without ever leaving (or being able to leave) this limited, or as Kierkegaard prefers to say, "finite" one. There are intriguing similarities here to Heidegger's notion that it is "language itself which speaks." As for Heidegger, language and speech remind Kierkegaard of the activities of "building and dwelling."[15]

To build up means, then, to construct something from the ground up into the heights. This *up* [*op*] certainly points to the heights, but only when the height also means the opposite—depth—do we say build up![16]

The secret of that strange word "edify" (*opbygge*) can be found in the familiar word, "build up" (*opbygge*). In what some might find a mock performance of ordinary language analysis, Kierkegaard attempts to clarify the proper use of "build up" according to its usage by the man in the street. Once he has discovered how *opbygge* is used when it refers to the activity of constructing dwellings (edifices), then he will be ready to understand the more ambiguous cases in which it refers to "edification." And he decides, after careful examination, that *opbygge* can only mean "build up" and not "build on" or "next to," that it refers qualitatively and not quantitatively to building because the prefix *op* makes explicitly clear an original act of vertical construction. Kierkegaard's study of the familiar use of *opbygge* shows him that all instances in which vertical building takes place make it clear that "building is from the ground up." This leads him to recognize in *op-bygge* the corresponding activity of digging down to make a foundation for building up. Hence, *opbygge* means both height and depth; means the proportional relationships between the visible part and the less visible foundation. Together, he says, they tell us something about what is fundamental to "building up."

As Kierkegaard repeats the word *opbygge*, finding its dimensions and qualities, he makes it sound stranger and stranger. And while he practices this repetition, he brings into the discourse a whole family of related *op* words so that they too might share in this inversion of the familiar becoming strange. This family resemblance includes: *opelsker* (foster), *opdrage* (upbringing), *opfordre* (challenge), *opdage* (discover), to mention a few. Each of these words gains force and begins to take on some of the qualities of the transferred term *opbygge* since each seems now to have both a commonplace (familiar, presumed) and rather unusual or hidden (strange) meaning. By the time Kierkegaard shifts back to *opbygge*, edify, the familiar has become strange and the strange begins to sound somewhat familiar.

The two meanings of the word *opbygge* transfer us back and forth across the limits of the strange and familiar and, in the convergence of other *op* words with *opbygge*, Kierkegaard manages to get *opbygge* to hover almost magically as the symbolic embodiment of a language of limits. This hovering of *opbygge* may be precisely a case of what it means to edify. An edifying speech awakens the listener by evoking a sense of contrast between the relative density or magnitude of two dimensions of meaning. And just as metaphor, by creating a field of contrast, releases us from the captivity of confined meanings to the surprise of new ones, so an edifying discourse has the capacity to renew our concern for what is of ultimate value, that we may once again (or even for the first time) arrive at the threshold of choice. Having brought the reader to this threshold, Kierkegaard then "reaches through" this metaphorical utterance become symbol, finding in that symbol a comparison to Christian love, the love of the neighbor, the love in which the familiar and the strange draw closer together in establishing affinities, as a person goes over to encounter a stranger.[17]

In the self-neighbor relationship metaphorical speaking becomes metaphor in the flesh: first, because in the love of the neighbor like and unlike are united, and, second, this reaching out to the stranger (as to oneself) reveals the hidden meaning of Christ's life. The individual enacts a likeness to the Divine Presence corresponding to the divine having become humanlike in the God-Man. To find oneself where one least expected, in the unfamiliar, the neighbor who is simply "nearby," is a lesson in surprises transcending the idea of development as self-discovery, self-identity, or self-improvement. The real test of love consists in the response to the call of likeness in the most unlike, the neighbor, the one whose "dwelling in nearness" (*naerboende*) is not conceived in spatial distance but temporally as the near in time, as one's contemporary. As contemporaries, the neighbors nevertheless abide in their differences. They do not become alike but find each other in and through their differences, find themselves by means of this difference. The meaning of self becomes strange when self-love is to be reflected in the love of the unfamiliar. The sense of self is accordingly strained and, says Kierkegaard, the neighbor provides the opportunity for the discovery that God is the "middle term" in the I-Thou relationship: an intermediary who comes to presence in the joining of self and neighbor.

In the word *opbygge* Kierkegaard discovers a metaphor of his vocation: an upbuilding, an edifying game played in earnest, as children play "stranger" with the old and familiar.[18] How then should the vocation of one who seeks to praise love be understood? How far does Kierkegaard's loving language allow us to enter into this edifying game?

If love builds up, through each act of speaking it modifies, by presupposing that love is already present in the other(s), then, says Kierkegaard, love works through restraint and secrecy. It is a strange phenomenon that one who instructs, leads, or guides does so through an assumption that makes a silence in his speaking and an expectation brought through a presupposition. That person does not point to himself as source of power (*Grundvold*, foundation), nor does he direct attention solely to the external object of discourse. He informs "with a glance" that fixes the possibility of a building up. Still, says Kierkegaard, "love is never completely present in any person," and we are inclined to seek the flaw or frailty whose removal (by us) should lead to the perfection of abilities. This is again a disproportionate relationship between man and man. If one aims to be or claims to be responsible for the building up in another, then the groundwork is removed and the transformation one-sided, therefore incomplete in actuality. The work of love requires self-renunciation. How can we understand self-renunciation in this context?

Is what Kierkegaard tells us here to be understood simply as Christian doctrine evolved curiously out of transferred language? If we translate the whole story into an ordinary, though highly valued situation we have the following. There are individuals who speak to us in such a way that they call up confidence and conviction in our own process of becoming a whole integrated person. We feel that their expectations of us presuppose our own capabilities and growth and that they let us be ourselves, even while they instruct, guide, or explain. We feel free to be ourselves in their presence because they do not need to see us as different than we are. We feel built up through ourselves in their presence and many new things are possible for us to act on. They seem to have a way of focusing their speaking and listening so that their abilities and qualities are not an imposition. In the qualities and abilities belonging to each of us we are for ourselves; then there is something else that we have for one another—that is the work of love. Self-renunciation means that we make it unnecessary to project our wisdom, experience, and understanding on the other self, so that the other self shines through the opening. This means that we make ourselves a clearing place for others. "Love is not an exclusive characteristic, but it is a characteristic by which or in virtue of which you exist for others."[19] The paradox that slowly forms in the context of this kind of experiencing is the apparent paradox of Kierkegaard's words. If self-renunciation is the key to speaking that is letting be and loving forth, what kind of a speaking is it that explains this to us? There is a way of being our knowledge through self-renunciation; but is this not self-love, seemingly the opposite of Christian religiosity?

The kind of speaking which is simultaneously self-renunciation is discourse on love "which is love precisely by giving up the present moment and the immediate." For the speaker to win approval in that present moment is impossible, so impossible that he "should himself point out the misunderstanding" in the case that he might inadvertently win the approval of the present moment through his discourse.[20] To speak of love in such a way that it meets the approval of one's contemporaries, to please and gratify the congregation, to act poetically upon others and upon oneself is possible. Kierkegaard claims that this is really to be understood as "self-love" (*selvkjerlighed*). And we know from the *Papirer* that the example he had in mind was his contemporary N. F. S. Gruntvig, who referred to his followers as "the people of love."

In the section preceding the conclusion of *Works of Love* Kierkegaard faces head on the problem of "The Work of Love in Praising Love." There he draws the fundamental distinction between two kinds of communication: the one arising out of self-love, which is poetic, which aims to win the praise and approval of its own times, which stands on the basis of talent (genius); the other arising out of self-renunciation, which has sacrificial disinterestedness (*opofrende uegennyttighed*) as its characteristic, which relinquishes the present moment, is not publicly noticeable, and stands related to what is universal in mankind. It is in this context that Kierkegaard can say that one who praises art and science "emphasizes the cleavage between the talented and untalented among men."[21] But the one who praises love serves to equalize all, "not in common poverty nor in a common mediocrity, but in the community of the highest."

How should we understand this distinction between two kinds of speaking, especially if we take into account Kierkegaard's own (pseudonymous) description of the "style of the subjective thinker" in the *Postscript*? There the thinker (speaker) has "imagination and feeling, dialectics in existential inwardness, together with passion." He is "a dialectician dealing with the existential." He is not a man of science but an artist who uses the various spheres of existence (aesthetic, ethical, religious) to portray the art of existing interpenetrated with thought. But the subjective thinker is no one of these spheres; rather, they are at his disposal as materials through which to become concrete. "The subjective thinker has only a single scene, existence," and the reality of this is incommunicable in any direct form. Instead the subjective thinker (speaker) takes an ethical stand and presents "whatever is great in the sphere of the universally human" not as a subject for admiration, but "as an ethical requirement" which unfolds in the form of a possibility, though granted an ideal possibility which has as its focus the ideal of universality as human possibility.[22] The difference between direct (naive) and indirect (reflective) communication is that the latter is symbolic and requires interpretation and therefore an "appropriation process."

The poet's art and the art of the one who discourses are alike in the sense that the act of doing is precisely the act of saying. The one depends upon talent and is an art, the other requires no more than what is universally human and is therefore the work of each one. But Kierkegaard is himself too much of a poet for us to let this distinction pass unquestioned. Indeed, Kierkegaard makes the comparison yield only the finest of distinctions, for the poet's relationship to his source of inspiration, his muse, is very much like self-renunciation and prayer except that the poet wants to move in the direction of a result, namely, the poem, and has a jesting relationship toward the muse and the process by means of which the poem comes into being. In this way, the poet is a kind of medium or clearing for the happening of the poem and its voice. What then is the difference? Is not the poet's way a locating of the foundation (*Grundvolden*) through depth, through inwardness; a humility in relation to the source and a communication of praise? What could be more metaphoric and symbolic than the poet's indirect communication?

Repeated efforts, at the close of *Works of Love*, to state the difference between poetic and religious discourse pose, face to face, the finite and partial love of which the poet sings against the infinite and impartial love of the religious speaker's discourse. Having juxtaposed the two spheres of ordinary and extraordinary (Christian) forms of speech as one of inversions of value, and having called into question—indeed, alerted us—to the problem of locating the foundations upon which acts of human speech are built up, the further contrasting of poetic and religious speech, where both are supreme acts of metaphoric and imaginative unity, enables Kierkegaard, communicating as witness under his own name, to anticipate the reader's hesitation to believe in the content of the communication. Kierkegaard withdraws through the curtain of double reflection, leaving the reader with the last judgment about the discourse. He does this by casting suspicion on the sincerity of the speaker's motive to praise love, as if to say: "How much of this talk is really only poetry parading itself as devotional address?"

> If, then, one undertakes to praise love and is asked if it really is out of love on his part that he does it: the answer must be, "No other person can decide this accurately; possibly it is vanity, pride—in short, of evil—but it is also possible that it is love.[23]

The question of speaker's motive and speaker's act is turned back upon itself in the reflective tension of contrasting forms which itensifies the measure of the speaker's inwardness. In short, the discourse turns Socratic. In short, the poet's art becomes identical with the educator's concealment. But the "work of love" to which the loving language of the discourse bears witness is universalized as the work that everyone should do and, moreover, the work that everyone ultimately desires to do. The differences between individuals of uniqueness and talent in the sphere of finite distribution of human wealth are transformed in the infinite sphere as the unity of common task in the kingdom of abundance of meaning and spiritual plenitude.

The foundation of the possibility of edifying speech, like the foundation upon which the educator constructs the educative event, is an act of faith which makes the deepest generosity possible: the element that would ultimately complete the individual in a process of becoming is also one that belongs to him and that, paradoxically, he is in process of coming to possess. For Kierkegaard, this foundation of love requires self-sacrifice and detachment in relationship to others. Edification, the *opbyggelig*, requires sacrifice, the *opofrende*, if love is not to become pride, the *opblaest*. And Kierkegaard has clearly identified this act with Christianity itself, as living in the image of God; as being, like Christ, a servant. But Kierkegaard is not Christ, he is becoming a Christian. As an instrument of God, he is not God.

The great risk of the educator who practices indirect communication and who, more directly, seeks to bring his reader to edifying truths through self-renunciation, is the possibility of that author's becoming inexcessible, avoiding reciprocity, and finally withholding himself from the possibility of also becoming the beloved. In the distinction between the art and the work of praising love arises the problem of fundamental accessibility and mutuality for the speaker, Kierkegaard. So fearful is he of dominating his reader that he inadvertently dominates him by his concealment. Moreover, this tendency to be inaccessible to true mutuality is replicated in the tendency of Kierkegaard's discourse on love to place greatest emphasis on loving one's neighbor, that impossible other, and less on the importance of the reciprocity of love, the need and willingness to be loved. Communication in the spheres of the human and the divine are clearly parallel and interrelated for Kierkegaard. But the problem with love in the inter-human sphere, the sphere of ordinary communication, is mirrored by the problem of divine love.

At the conclusion of *Works of Love* Kierkegaard says, "To love human beings is the only true sign that you are a Christian. To love human beings is to love God and to love God is to love human beings; what you do unto men you do unto God, and therefore what you do unto men God does unto you." "God repeats with the intensification of infinity." Kierkegaard's God is like an echo to the individual's solitude. "But who believes in echo if night and day he lives in urban confusion?"[24]

The tremendous importance Kierkegaard attaches to love that expects no reward, unrequited love, and to the "like-for-like" of loving human beings and God as echoings of one's solitude, has as a further consequence the possibility that the reciprocal relationships are diminished. If the self is not responsible for the neighbor in reciprocal relationship according to the divine command, then the neighbor becomes "nothing but the stumbling block to prove one's own creative omnipotence as one of love."[25] The role of the beloved is devalued and what one finds is a return to the "erotic immediacy" of the aesthetic view where love is objectless—a return to A's "Echo." The other becomes merely a metaphor essentially characterized by deathlike aspects as in the absolute impossibility of reciprocity in the "work of love in remembering the dead."

In a world of urban confusion when it becomes increasingly difficult to see another as neighbor, and yet where the idea of love of one's neighbor includes no criteria for altering the setting of the world which makes realization of that love possible, what form of action remains? What form of speech? Does Kierkegaard's dialectic of communication suffer finally from a case of melancholy where fear of reciprocity is the fear of creating dependency relationship, of having misguided disciples? Does the only legitimate form of communication remain the concealment of a Socratic educator's smiling to himself that through unselfish and sacrificial (*opofrende*) acts he secretly participates with the other in an edifying (*opbyggelig*) education?

The love of which Kierkegaard speaks brings him, in one sense, beyond the Socratic, in celebrating the concrete universality of human becoming in the lesson of learning to love that which we have in common with one another—the unique value of human interiority as consciousness realizing its infinite source. Here lies the further though unexplored groundwork of authentic communality, an area into which Kierkegaard did not find sufficient access. In another sense, Kierkegaard maintains the maieutic position that the work of love requires an art of discourse which lovingly offers the difficulty of understanding as the reader's opportunity to appropriate a knowledge of love as indicative of a knowledge that transforms. Art and work, language and love, teacher and pupil remain in dialectical tension in an educative process that is essentially unfinished because it is devoted to the truth of human being as human becoming. The truth of human becoming requires metaphorical speech, language that continually calls for interpretation in the plenitude of its meanings.

> The communication of results is an unnatural form of intercourse between man and man, in so far as every man is a spiritual being, for whom *the truth consists in nothing else than the self-activity of personal appropriation*, which the communication of result tends to prevent.[26]

The imperfect Socrates stands for Kierkegaard as the embodiment of that self-activity of personal appropriation, as the emblem for his authorship. He is the imperfect educator, an analogy for the authorship and the limitations of its ability to make transformations in the reader: to inquire, to inform, and to seek to enable but never to cause the crucial action. Socrates is also the philosopher who prepares us, leads us up to the moment, smiles, and vanishes simultaneously as we leap. A witness, but also a limited witness who is not quite joined to the other through what is known. And this is the Kierkegaardian limit: to approach, to engage others in belonging through that which is made known, but to hold in reserve the final embrace, which is only for God— as if the embrace of human love would subdue the quest for the Divine. At the other end of the melancholy for which he, among other Danes, became famous is the reticent individual who sees himself fated to serve another order. Given the parameters of the authorship, its truth still holds. We cannot know what would complete us, nor can we complete one another. The educative motive that seeks perfection of self-knowledge and finality in its inward journey confronts the parody of its own strivings. Philosophy ends in humor. The celebration of this impasse is the story that the authorship tells about the education of human becoming and that makes Kierkegaard's many-sided authorship a dialectic of education.

Notes

Introduction

1. See Jens Himmelstrup, ed., *Soren Kierkegaard: International Bibliografi* (Copenhagen: Nyt Nordisk Forlag, 1962); Aage Jorgensen, *Soren Kierkegaard-literatur 1961-1970: En forelobig bibliografi* (Aarhus: Akademisk Boghandel, 1971); and Josiah Thompson, ed., *Kierkegaard, a Collection of Critical Essays*, Bibliographical Supplement (Garden City: Doubleday & Co., 1972).

2. Two recent books that explore themes unifying Kierkegaard's pseudonymous authorship are John W. Elrod, *Being and Existence in Kierkegaard's Pseudonymous Works* (Princeton: Princeton University Press, 1975); and Mark C. Taylor, *Kierkegaard's Pseudonymous Authorship: A Study of Time and the Self* (Princeton: Princeton University Press, 1975).

Part I

Preface

1. Soren Kierkegaard, *Concluding Unscientific Postscript*, trans. David F. Swenson and Walter Lowrie (Princeton: Princeton University Press, 1968), p. 81 (hereafter cited as *CUP*). Danish edition, *Soren Kierkegaard's Samlede Vaerker*, ed. A. B. Drachmann, J. L. Heiberg, and H. O. Lange, 15 vols., 2d ed. (Copenhagen: Gyldensalske Boghandel, 1920-1936), 7:79 (hereafter cited as *SV*).

2. Soren Kierkegaard, *Concept of Irony*, trans. Lee M. Capel (Bloomington: Indiana University Press, 1965), p. 255 (hereafter cited as *CI*).

3. *CI*, p. 50.

4. *The Point of View for My Work as an Author*, trans. Walter Lowrie (New York: Harper & Row, Harper Torchbooks, 1962), p. 75 (hereafter cited as *PV*).

5. *PV*, p. 29.

6. *PV*, p. 75.

1: Socrates Hovering

1. G. W. F. Hegel, *Lectures on the History of Philosophy*, vol. 1, trans. E. S. Haldane (New York: The Humanities Press, 1963), p. 387 (hereafter cited as *HP*).

2. *HP*, p. 396.

3. *HP*, p. 400.

4. *HP*, p. 401.

5. *HP*, p. 403.

6. *HP*, p. 405.

7. *HP*, chap. 2, B, 1c.

8. *HP*, p. 408.

9. *HP*, p. 446.

10. *CI*, p. 245.

11. *CI*, p. 254.

12. *CI*, p. 287.

13. *CI*, p. 242.

14. *CI*, p. 286.

15. *CI*, p. 85n. "The ironist raises the individual out of immediate existence, and this is his emancipating function; but thereafter he lets him *hover* like the coffin of Mohammed, which, according to legend, is suspended between two magnets—attraction and repulsion."

16. *CI*, p. 278.

17. *CI*, p. 79.

18. *CI*, p. 202.

19. *CI*, p. 88.

20. *CI*, p. 203.

2: Socrates Vanishing

1. Soren Kierkegaard, *Philosophical Fragments*, trans. David F. Swenson (Princeton: Princeton University Press, 1962), p. 12 (hereafter cited as *PF*). *SV*, 4:204.

2. *PF*, p. 13. *SV* 4:205.

3. *PF*, p. 37. *SV* 4:223.

4. Francis Macdonald Cornford, *The Origin of Attic Comedy* (Gloucester: Peter Smith, 1968), p. 139.

5. *CUP*, p. 279. *SV* 7:303.

6. *PF*, p. 91. *SV*, 4:266.

7. *CUP*, p. 176. *SV*, 7:183.

8. *CUP*, p. 182. *SV*, 7:190.

9. *CUP*, p. 182. *SV*, 7:190.

10. Soren Kierkegaard, *The Sickness Unto Death*, trans. Walter Lowrie (Princeton: Princeton University Press, 1968), p. 147 (hereafter cited as *SUD*). *SV*, 11:145.

11. Aristotle *Nichomachean Ethics*, 1126-1127, trans. W. D. Ross, in *Introduction to Aristotle*, ed. Richard McKeon (New York: Modern Library, 1947).

12. *CI*, p. 97. *SV*, 13:167.

13. *CUP*, p. 184. *SV*, 7:191.

14. *PF*, p. 28. *SV*, 4:216.

15. *CI*, p. 278. *SV*, 13:362.

16. *CUP*, p. 491. *SV*, 7:544.

17. *CUP*, p. 490. *SV*, 7:540.

18. Julius Schousboe, *Om Begrebet Humor hos S. K.* (Copenhagen: Arnold Busck, 1925), p. 26.

19. Harald Hoffding, *Den Store Humor* (Copenhagen: Gyldendals, 1916; reprint ed., 1967), p. 69.

20. *CUP*, p. 184. *SV*, 7:191.

3: Socrates Witnessing

1. *Soren Kierkegaards Papirer*, ed. P. A. Heiberg, V. Kuhr, and E. Torsting, 11 vols. in 18 parts (Copenhagen: Gyldendalske Boghandel Nordisk Forlag, 1909-1948, vol. X¹, Part A, entry 235 (hereafter cited as *Papirer*, then by volume number, part, and entry number; hence this reference becomes X¹ A 235).

2. Soren Kierkegaard, *Works of Love*, trans. Howard V. and Edna H. Hong (New York: Harper & Row, Harper Torchbooks, 1964), p. 256 (hereafter cited as *WOL*). Danish edition, *Samlede Vaerker*, ed. A. B. Drachmann, J. L. Heiberg, and H. O. Lange (1920-36; reprint ed. supervised by Peter P. Rodhe, 20 vols., Copenhagen: Gyldendalske Boghandel Nordisk Forlag, 1962-1964) 12:263. (Since this is the only instance where I will be using the reprint ed., references will be to its title, *Kjerlighedens Gjerninger*, cited as *KG*.)

3. *WOL*, p. 256. *KG*, p. 263.

4. *WOL*, p. 258. *KG*, p. 265.

5. *PV*, p. 143. *SV*, 13:523.

6. *PV*, p. 147. *SV*, 13:528.

7. *PV*, p. 144. *SV*, 13:528.

8. *PV*, p. 144. *SV*, 13:528.

9. *PV*, p. 144. *SV*, 13:528.

10. *PV*, p. 135. *SV*, 13:647.

11. *PV*, p. 136. *SV*, 13:651.

12. *PV*, Preface, p. 107. *SV*, 13:631.

13. Plato *Gorgias* 521d-c, trans. Woodhead, from *Socratic Dialogues* (Edinburgh: The Nelson Press, 1953).

14. *Gorgias* 472c.

15. *PV*, p. 135. *SV*, 13:647.

16. *PV*, p. 134. *SV*, 13:646.

17. *PV*, p. 41. *SV*, 13:590.

18. *PV*, p. 131. *SV*, 13:646.

19. *PV*, p. 131. *SV*, 13:646.

Part II

Preface

1. Soren Kierkegaard, *Either/Or*, vol. 1, trans. David F. Swenson and Lillian Marvin Swenson (Garden City: Anchor Books, 1959), p. 14 (hereafter cited as *E/O*, 1).

2. *E/O*, 1:195.

4: A Revealing Education

1. Soren Kierkegaard, *Either/Or*, vol. 2, trans. Walter Lowrie (Garden City: Anchor Books, 1959), p. 178 (hereafter cited as *E/O*, 2).

2. *E/O*, 2:210.

3. *E/O*, 2:327.

4. *E/O*, 2:182.

5. *E/O*, 2:185-188.

6. See Eduard Geismar, *Soren Kierkegaard, Hans Livsudvikling og For-fattervirksomhed*, 6 vols. (Copenhagen: G. E. C. Gads Forlag, 1927-28), 1:53.

7. *E/O*, 2:194.

8. *E/O*, 2:195.

9. *E/O*, 2:333.

10. *E/O*, 2:264.

11. *E/O*, 2:214.

12. *E/O*, 2:210.

13. *E/O*, 2:215.
14. *E/O*, 2:215.
15. *E/O*, 2:217.
16. *E/O*, 2:220.
17. *E/O*, 2:221.
18. *E/O*, 2:220.
19. *E/O*, 2:220.
20. *E/O*, 2:220.
21. *E/O*, 2:331.
22. *E/O*, 2:337.

5: The Character of an Educator

1. *E/O*, 2:164.
2. *E/O*, 2:228.
3. *E/O*, 2:274.
4. *E/O*, 2:277.
5. *E/O*, 2:273.
6. *E/O*, 2:271.
7. *E/O*, 2:277.
8. *E/O*, 2:242.

6: Finding the Perfect Limit

1. *E/O*, 1:143.
2. *E/O*, 1:144.
3. Cf. Gregor Malantschuk, *Dialektik og Eksistens hos Soren Kierke-gaard* (Copenhagen: Hans Reitzels Forlag, 1968), p. 212; eds. and trans. Howard V. and Edna H. Hong, *Kierkegaard's Thought* (Princeton: Princeton University Press, 1971), p. 221.
4. *E/O*, 1:155.
5. *E/O*, 2:12.
6. *E/O*, 1:150.
7. *E/O*, 1:150.
8. *E/O*, 1:137.
9. *E/O*, 1:138.
10. *E/O*, 1:141.
11. *E/O*, 1:144.
12. *E/O*, 1:146.
13. *E/O*, 1:159.
14. *E/O*, 1:157.
15. *E/O*, 1:151.

16. *E/O*, 1:288.
17. *E/O*, 1:296.

7: Educating Consciousness at a Limit

1. Immanuel Kant, *Metaphysical Foundation of Morals*, trans. Carl J. Friedrich, in *The Philosophy of Kant, Moral and Political Writings* (New York: Modern Library), p. 181.
2. Immanuel Kant, *Metaphysical Foundation of Morals*, quoted from H. J. Paton, *Categorical Imperative* (London: Hutchinson University Library, 1953), p. 185.
3. Immanuel Kant, *Critique of Practical Reason*, trans. Lewis White Beck (New York: The Bobbs-Merrill Company, 1956), p. 156.
4. Ibid., p. 123.
5. Ibid, p. 158.
6. *E/O*, 2:350.
7. *E/O*, 2:351.
8. *E/O*, 2:356.
9. *Papirer*, 4 B 59.

8: Either/Or: An Eventful Education

1. *E/O*, 2:183, 184, 178.
2. *E/O*, 2:255.
3. Benjamin D. Wright and Shirley A. Tuska, "The Childhood Romance Theory of Teacher Development," *The School Review* 75, 2 (1967): 123-154.
4. Ibid.

Part III

Preface

1. *Papirer*, VIII² B 81.
2. Ibid.

9: Eventful Discourse

1. *CUP*, p. 473.
2. *CUP*, p. 473.

3. *CUP*, p. 506.

4. *CUP*, p. 507.

5. *PF*, chap. 2.

6. Cf. Malantschuk, *Dialektik og Eksistens*, p. 140.

7. *CUP*, p. 107.

8. *CUP*, p. 111.

9. Cf. *Papirer*, X² A 235.

10. James Collins, *The Mind of Kierkegaard* (Chicago: Henry Regnery Co., 1953), p. 154.

11. *Papirer*, VIII² B 81.

12. Erich Frank, *Philosophical Understanding and Religious Truth* (New York: Oxford University Press, 1966), p. 76.

13. *CUP*, p. 277.

14. *CUP*, p. 306.

10: The Limits of Language

1. *PV*, p. 15.

2. Soren Kierkegaard, *Edifying Discourses*, trans. David F. Swenson and Lillian Marvin Swenson, 4 vols. (Minneapolis: Augsburg Publishing House, 1943-46), vol. 4.

3. *Papirer*, XI² A 37.

4. *E/O*, 1:41.

5. *E/O*, 1:33.

6. Cf. Albert Hofstadter, "Art: Death and Transfiguration, A Study in Hegel's Theory of Romanticism," *Review of National Literatures* 1 (1970): 149-164.

7. *E/O*, 1:64.

11. The Language of Limits

1. *WOL*, p. 199. *KG*, p. 203.

2. *WOL*, p. 40. *KG*, p. 29.

3. *WOL*, p. 19. *KG*, p. 9.

4. *WOL*, p. 29. *KG*, p. 17.

5. *WOL*, p. 32. *KG*, p. 21.

6. *WOL*, p. 66. *KG*, p. 58.

7. *WOL*, p. 67. *KG*, p. 58.

8. *WOL*, p. 199. *KG*, p. 203.

9. *Papirer*, X¹ A 235.

10. *Papirer*, VIII² B 83. I have accepted the Hongs' translation here in their important editions of *Kierkegaard's Journals and Papers*, ed. and

trans. Howard V. and Edna H. Hong, 4 vols (Bloomington: Indiana University Press, 1967-1976), 2:281 (hereafter cited as *J&P*).

11. *WOL*, p. 206. *KG*, p. 210.

12. *Papirer*, VIII² B 85. *J&P*, 1:283.

13. *WOL*, p. 199. *KG*, p. 203.

14. Philip Wheelwright, *Metaphor and Reality* (Bloomington: Indiana University Press, 1962), p. 70.

15. Martin Heidegger, "Building Dwelling Thinking," *Poetry, Language, Thought*, trans. Albert Hofstadter (New York: Harper & Row, 1971). A strikingly similar exploration of language is undertaken by Heidegger through looking at the German *Bauen*, which discloses the meaning of dwelling, neighbor, gods, mortals, etc. Heidegger does not make explicit reference to metaphor, but he goes on to speak about "bridges."

16. *WOL*, p. 201. *KG*, p. 205.

17. *WOL*, pp. 340-342 and Part One, chap. 2. *KG*, pp. 353-354.

18. *WOL*, p. 200. *KG*, p. 204.

19. *WOL*, p. 211. *KG*, p. 216.

20. *WOL*, p. 339. *KG*, p. 352.

21. *WOL*, p. 335. *KG*, p. 347.

22. *CUP*, p. 312.

23. *WOL*, p. 343. *KG*, p. 357.

24. *WOL*, p. 352. *KG*, p. 366.

25. T. W. Adorno, "On Kierkegaard's Doctrine of Love," *Studies in Philosophy and Social Science*, 8 (1940): 413-429.

26. *CUP*, p. 217.

Index